The BreakBeat Poets Volume 2

Black Girl Magic

Edited by
Mahogany L. Browne
Idrissa Simmonds
Jamila Woods

H

Haymarket Books
Chicago, Illinois

Published in 2018 by
Haymarket Books
P.O. Box 180165
Chicago, IL 60618
773-583-7884
www.haymarketbooks.org
info@haymarketbooks.org

ISBN: 978-1-60846-857-7

Trade distribution:
In the US, Consortium Book Sales and Distribution, www.cbsd.com
In Canada, Publishers Group Canada, www.pgcbooks.ca
In the UK, Turnaround Publisher Services, www.turnaround-uk.com
All other countries, Ingram Publisher Services International,
IPS_Intlsales@ingramcontent.com

This book was published with the generous support of Lannan Foundation
and Wallace Action Fund.

Printed in Canada by union labor.

Library of Congress Cataloging-in-Publication data is available.

Cover art, "Chocolate Lady" by Brianna McCarthy.
Cover design by Brett Neiman.

10 9 8 7 6 5 4 3

Contents

I'M BLACK   21

The first thing you do is to forget that I'm Black.
Second, you must never forget that I'm Black.

—Pat Parker

SHARPENING MY OYSTER KNIFE   41

I do not weep at the world—I am too busy sharpening my oyster knife.
—Zora Neale Hurston

DUTY TO FIGHT 59

It is our duty to fight for our freedom. It is our duty to win.
We must love each other and support each other. We have
nothing to lose but our chains.

—Assata Shakur

ALL THE EVENTS THAT HAPPEN TO YOU 81

You may not control all the events that happen to you,
but you can decide not to be reduced by them.

—Maya Angelou

WRONG IS NOT MY NAME   **109**

I am not wrong: Wrong is not my name
My name is my own my own
my own

—June Jordan

A NEW PERSON   129

I was a new person then,
I knew things I had not known before,
I knew things that you can know only if you have been through
    what I had just been through.

—Jamaica Kincaid

SOMETHING HAS TRIED TO KILL ME AND HAS FAILED

come celebrate
with me that everyday
something has tried to kill me
and has failed.

—Lucille Clifton

I want to look happily forward. I want to be optimistic. I want to have a dream. I want to live in jubilee. I want my daughters to feel that they have the power to at least try to change things, even in a world that resists change with more strength than they have.

—Edwidge Danticat

Index of Poets

Foreword

Patricia Smith

Almost thirty years ago, I wrote a poem that stumbled toward explaining my unsteady root in the world. I was weary of scratching out life under a microscope, of having that life dissected, defined, and ultimately dismissed by others. When I sat down to scrawl this thick stanza, with its single capital letter and breathless progression, I was both fed up with explaining and desperately craving an explanation.

What It's Like to Be a Black Girl (For Those Of You Who Aren't)

First of all, it's being 9 years old and
feeling like you're not finished, like your
edges are wild, like there's something,
everything, wrong. it's dropping food
coloring in your eyes to make them blue and suffering
their burn in silence. it's popping a bleached
white mop head over the kinks of your hair and
priming in front of the mirrors that deny your
reflection. it's finding a space between your
legs, a disturbance in your chest, and not knowing
what to do with the whistles. it's jumping
double dutch until your legs pop, it's sweat
and vaseline and bullets, it's growing tall and
wearing a lot of white, it's smelling blood in
your breakfast, it's learning to say *fuck* with
grace but learning to fuck without it, it's
flame and fists and life according to motown,
it's finally having a man reach out for you
then caving in
around his fingers.

At nine, all I craved to be was "other." I prayed that blue-black, nappy and female was a temporary malady, that the West Side of Chicago was just a training ground for the wider world—the world presented as a dreamily whitewashed dreamscape that I never doubted represented a reality just outside my reach.

Even my mother, my guidance, urged me to crave who I wasn't. As an answer to "Who am I, really?" I was plopped down in front of our big floor model Philco to watch a succession of television shows featuring several hundred carefully framed lives I was urged to aspire to. When my mother was done cackling at the goofiness of Lucille Ball or professing Walter Cronkite a god of sorts, I flipped channels. I flipped channels, searching American faces, listening to American conversations, peeking into American homes. Of course, I never found a Black girl.

No voices sounded like mine, so every plummet and rise in my song was wrong somehow. No faces looked like mine, and I despised the mirror for its inability to utter the lies I needed to hear. In the world I was being taught was the right one, no streets, no neighborhoods, no schools, no mothers looked anything like mine.

So I turned away from the babbling broadcasts and began to wait. I waited patiently for a peculiar and impossible magic, that sweep of the wand that would lift me from the baffling throes of little Black girl-dom and into the righteous, much easier existence awaiting me.

Meanwhile, my nose was too broad, my hair too crinkled. I clutched shameful stories of a mother from Alabama, a daddy from Arkansas, and their loud way with double negatives. I lived in a tenement hovel where roaches dropped from the ceiling into my bed and mice got trapped inside the stove. That hovel happened to be on the West Side of Chicago, the side of town everybody warned you to stay away from. And the school was one of the worst in the city. And, from the woman purporting to be my rock: *For Jesus' sake, girl, talk right like you got some sense. If you ever want to get out of this neighborhood, ever, you got to fix your tongue and talk right, like white people, you got to talk about stuff white folks talk about, you got to say things white folks want to hear. And Lord, I don't know why your nose so wide, none of my people got noses like that. And I can't even drag a comb through that nappy hair.*

What I was was not enough. I was wrong, I needed correction. I was to become a scrubbed slate, detached from my own history. If I was to

have any story at all, I had to grant anyone and everyone else permission xix
to write it—any beginning, any middle, any outcome.

I was Black and female. As such, I was taught that the world would
tell me what and who I was. What we are.

We are the color pulsing beneath the closed eye, the tinge of a room
at moonfall, we are steady suspect since we share our hue with the night.
Because we are never seen clearly—consistently spied-upon through
a safely-distanced shroud—we are diminished, trivialized, spoken of
as stain. We are the rollicking hips and the curious hair, the bristling
oddity, the tangled waft of shea and spiced oil, the throats that refuse to
constrict. Everyone has had a go at us, poking fervently at spaces in our
spirit, plumping us for consumption, starving us for spectacle, killing us
for sport. We're seen as the blaring gold tooth, the tangling weave, the
ungrammatical phrase, the public exhibition, the occasional inconvenient
corpse. We are objectified, analyzed, and rearranged to fit someone else's
perception of what a voiceless woman should be.

How curious it be, the obsession with reviling and renaming the
Black girl. How staggering our resistance. How maddening our sublime
propensity for magic—not a magic designed to pull us out of our own
bodies to become "the other," but a magic that would help us know
ourselves. And be glorified in the knowledge.

What you hold in your hands is not an anthology of verse, it is a
manual of glorious sorcery. It's page upon page upon page of stanza as
incantation—crafted not to make Black girls' lives less impenetrable and
lyrically palatable for the curious, but to revel in the chilling power of our
weaponry. This is not a guidebook for those skulking outside the circle
of our bewitched coven seeking to "understand" or "relate." This is not a
glimpse at our vulnerabilities, since—and I understand this may come as
a surprise to quite a few people—for all practical purpose, we have none.

These pages are not populated by *a* Black girl, not a single, all-
encompassing icon, but all of us—spewing pointed curses from Brooklyn,
Philly and Queens, DC and Kentucky, casting spells from the Chi and
the City of Angels, chanting ritually from the ATL, Minneapolis and
pinpoints in the Caribbean. We are immigrant, displaced, rattled,
resolute, resilient. We mourn men and mothers, grieve the passage of
time, walk taller and resolute through that old white world.

I relentlessly love my sisters. We have taken back the right to name ourselves. We have realized the unwavering strength in our hue, in our connections to each other, in stories that parallel and collide, in stanzas that all work toward revelation. We have finally discovered our second throat, the one that's propped wide open, the one that spews necessary expletives and wails runaway gospel. It's the throat they didn't want us to discover. Because there is no way it can be controlled.

As the poet Ariana Brown asks, ". . . in what version of the story do black women win?"

Here. This version. Here's where we win on every damn page—every page of this somber, celebratory narrative. Every page asks a question of our lives.

And just like magic, we have all the answers.

women win? i'm not always preparing
for war, but if you'll excuse me,
i'm always preparing for war.

How do we lose our own voices?

Introduction

My sister-in-law, whom I call my sister, is what most would like to call a "firecracker." She married my youngest brother, born to a father that was married to my mother lifetimes before, and we've been kin ever since. Whatever she says, it's usually with a snap of her eyes, a cut of her lips, or a finger wag. It is not a performance of Blackness; she is a Black woman. And these movements are hers, just like they were her mother's, just like they were her grandmother's—a tradition of survival. She's learned how to get her point across neatly: a knife in a drawer full of spoons. She's always accused of being too "rough" on people—which is where our sisterhood thickens, molasses strong.

I too have lived on that block, in that house, first door to the right, and you could find me: Angry Black Girl/Strong Black Girl/Black Girl You Call on When You Need to Get Things Done.

My sister, T, is too this woman; unapologetically, listening to Beyoncé with her three Black daughters and her eldest Black son. Praying faithfully for forgiveness, because she's begun to believe that she is hard to love. T, who snaps her eyes when pointing across the room, need not pray for forgiveness, I say. But it's hard to believe someone like me, especially when the world is fixed on telling her how strong and loud and wrong she is. I introduce to her June Jordan's mantra "I am not wrong/wrong is not my name," and we weep a little between laughter. These are moments I hold close to my chest. The phone glued to my ear as we cackle between shit talk and ferocious laughter.

Where in the world do they love a Black girl for being herself? We are primed to bear witness to Kardashians and Jenners pretending to be Black women with their cornrows and Black boyfriends. Their acrylics beaming under the hot light, the world their stage. No one asks them to settle down their finger snaps or tone down their hair color. No one judges them for their sexual partners or the sex tapes they leak. Their children are born, revered as beautiful, receive rightfully the world's love. They are offered modeling contracts and makeup deals like candy, as we sit by idly, college tuition debt growing, as our children die from lead poisoning in Flint, or Skittles in Florida, or because of disobedience in Maryland, or sleeping quietly on the family couch in Michigan.

Where in the world do they love a Black girl for being herself? When a twenty-seven-year-old activist can die after her second child is born due to cardiac arrest, her weight and height and eating patterns blamed for her health, but never the stress it must've caused her heart to watch her father ripped from this earth on repeat in high-def display; a reminder that Black death is the only thing certain and ours. Her name, so closely linked to the ghost of her father, Erica; a chant no one will sing until she is gone. My sister T is not my blood sister. But she is mine. She is me. We are one and the same when we love how we love, our teeth bared and gleaming, because we've grown to understand "I love you" as a weapon held against our throats. We retreat into ourselves and fight others trying to kill us: family members, friends, neighbors, and supervisors. We understand the small deaths (TV shows where all you see are jokes about us; weaves overpriced and deemed out of style until a hashtag with Gigi the newest trendsetter mimics a Black girl from IG; or the men we love disposing of us with statements of "too much" falling from their open palms) can culminate into an ultimate death. A death where there is no room for the love of ourselves, beginning the journey of void-filling through addiction, dangerous surgeries, and loneliness, though we oftentimes find ourselves unfolding to protect those same hands during vigils, protests, and rallies. This is what Black women have been taught to do: love and show up for what love has survived. And so, we do. Let those that look like us, take from us, until there is nothing left. We understand we are the backbone despite the backhand. And we love with the harshest tongues, believing that the survivors of such a spectacle are here to stay. We share intimacy this way, in hopes that if you see combat for affection, maybe you too will swing in the protection of our names.

But this is not a fail-proof plan. This is not the blueprint for home. For many years, I believed it was our only heirloom. To speak as hard as you love. I spoke to T today. I told her about the importance of apologizing. She sighs and cuts me off: "I meant it Sister, I'm not sorry." And I hear me ten years before. Angry and seething and righteous. I reply: "It's not about being right. You are not apologizing for what you believe to be true, you are apologizing for your hand in hurting someone else."

We hang up soon after and I am spinning, because while I ask my sister to do things I wasn't capable of doing at her age, I wish I'd had someone tell me about the power of forgiveness of myself. I believe we have the right to be snarky and witty and throw shade, if we choose. We owe ourselves the right to speak through a world that's tried to mute us all of our lives. But I know the difference between intention and impact. We've seen this before. And so we lash out, because we know our very lives are in danger. Elder Zora Neale Hurston wrote, "If you are silent about your pain, they'll kill you and say you enjoyed it." Eleanor Bumpurs, Korryn Gaines, Tanisha Anderson, Yvette Smith, Miriam Carey, Malissa Williams, Sandra Bland, and Rekia Boyd: killed for standing up, sitting down, speaking back, protecting their children, or just being Black women.

I believe with my whole self: ain't no room for a Black woman's voice to be policed. Our worth is always up for debate. My sister is one of the kindest women I know. I have witnessed her crumble to the ground in fear for her child and reach into her deepest pocket for grace when dealing with the graceless. A Black woman is often asked to lead (silently), to be the symbol of civility while everyone else plays from a different playbook, mocking her existence the entire time. T is the woman I dreamed of becoming. The way she rides for my little brother; their marriage is a fortress of forgiveness and love, the way it stretches until there is room for all of their children and dreams.

T sends me a text about being hard to love and I want to cry. Such a folktale: being hard to love. What a fable we've grown to believe as the rule. T is so easy to love. We are so easy to love. Our resilience and expansion is proof that magic exists. We are magic. We are Black girls grown into women, growing men and women, and in this collection of Black Girl Magicians are mantras, prayers, and promises of our survival. This anthology is a literary but breathing example of our great-great-great-great grandmothers' triumphant and explosive war cry.

Mahogany L. Browne

Introduction

To pull the phrase *blackgirlmagic* apart into its singular elements:

Black—the color of my kin. Of opal. Of beauty that is often de-centered, disregarded: holiness passed for evil.

Girl—a term used by Black women since the beginnings of Black women in reference and reverence to our homegirls.

Magic—rituals of persistence. Conjuring. Reclamation and possibility. Hope, survival, thriving, centering on our power and sisterhood and joy.

When a Black woman dares to speak her truth, she redefines understandings of womanhood.

Her voice echoes out, disrupting and delegitimizing tired stereotypes and tropes.

In short, there is magic.

Before Lupita had us raise our voices in collective jubilation as she grasped an Oscar between both hands—before Beyoncé brought a visual celebration of Black womanhood to the mainstream with *Lemonade*—before Ava DuVernay brought us *Middle of Nowhere* and *Selma*—before Issa Rae became the first Black woman to produce and direct her own show on HBO—before Serena solidified her status as the undisputed greatest of all time—I watched my mother pick her Afro towards the sun and rim her lips with red Revlon lipstick.

I watched her dot Chanel No. 5 behind her ears, grasp my brother and I each in one of her well-oiled hands, and walk out of our grandmother's home in East New York to the A at Euclid Avenue. She did this every day, entering the world with the tools she had at the time: prayer, a few phrases of her mother's kreyol to guard her spirit, and a wicked sense of style. Her life was specific and small and hers: nothing of note to anyone who could not bother to look closer. But I understood something about the way she inhabited her body and the space around it; that some rare magic was at play that enabled her to stride through a world hostile to Black women.

I should be clear: Black women are not superheroes. We hurt and bleed and are vulnerable and tired and fed up with all the shit. The tropes of Black women's strength and resilience, while often meant to uplift, can dehumanize and take away our ability to be seen as complex humans in need of tenderness. But—our ability to defy, persist, and excel in the face of systemic oppression is a magical beast. This ability does warrant examination, upliftment, and, yes, a hashtag.

Black girl magic is a qualifying term: it centers a conjuring that is specific to the Black woman—which means it is as rich and varied and impossible to define in singular terms as we are. We work, laugh, and exist amidst a racist cultural dissonance that is oddly disembodying: Black women writers, visual artists, academics, business and tech leaders, scientists and athletes are experiencing a noteworthy level of mainstream shine. We populate bestseller lists and reach millions on social media. Our thinking is sought out for panels and keynotes. We see our style grossly pilfered and distorted through the lens of whiteness. And still— alongside all this we have seen Rekia Boyd, Renisha McBride, Sandra Bland, Charleena Lyles, Korryn Gaines, Tarika Wilson, and countless others whose names we will never know lose their lives to the failure of the white imagination to police itself.* Black trans women are lost to disproportionately high rates of murder and violence. Years after the kidnapping of Nigerian school girls by Boko Haram terrorists, the social media call of "bring back our girls" has quieted to nothing.

What do we do in the face of this dissonance? What we have always done, my loves: continue the work of healing and holding one another. Others may or may not come along: no matter. The writing collected in these pages centers the ability of Black women to trust in our own possibility.

I was honored to touch these poems. I came to this anthology through the bond of sisterhood. Fitting that Mahogany should invite me to cofacilitate its creation along with Jamila, when the resilience, possibility, and love of Black womanhood have colored our friendship and my relationship to Black women in general. My childhood memories are full of red fingernails against Black hands and the work these hands did to pour life into children and one another. The dresser tops of my mother and her sisters were loaded with their version of potions: perfumes, compacts, pincushions grown stained and soft with use, family photos of our living and dead holding space next to cosmetics and Sunday prayer missiles. This is the alchemy that colors my writing and my personal definitions of

---

* "Because white men can't police their imagination black men are dying": haiku by the poet Claudia Rankine after visiting Ferguson, Missouri.

Black womanhood: ancestry, spirituality, flyness. I believed these women possessed magic due to their talent at harnessing possibility through staggering loss. I learned from their ability to be vulnerable, messy, and authentic in the face of personal tragedy and institutional injustice. The daily rituals the women in my family practiced to arm themselves before entering the world inform my approach to craft.

And what is crafting a good poem but the conjuring of magic? The words in this anthology transcend and transform imagination, even when describing the concrete realities of life. These pages hold the fullness of the diaspora, of language, of gender identity, of erotic love, and of sisterhood. The lack of a singular definition is what makes Black girl magic an essential topic of exploration. We are expansive. Through explorations of religion and motherhood, sex and love, relationships and ancestry, and lust, each artist gives new ways for thinking about Black girl magic. These poems, whether contemplating colorism on a tanning bed, exploring the intimacy of Black women tending to one another's heads, or moments of violence between Black women, are told with specificity and honesty. As editors, we sought poems that were unafraid to look head on. Poems that are uncomfortable, intimate, and striking.

Fannie Lou Hamer once said: "Sometimes it seem like to tell the truth today is to run the risk of being killed. But if I fall, I'll fall five feet four inches forward in the fight for freedom. I'm not backing off."

Hamer's words are in the context of the movement for Black people to gain voting rights in the United States, but they speak to a larger truth: whenever a Black woman dares to tell the truth about herself, to "remember her own memories"—to paraphrase Lucille Clifton—there is risk. Because we are seen as inherently dangerous, there is a threat any time we dare to be truthful about the abundance of our lives. To read the work of the women gathered in the pages of this anthology is to revel in and celebrate this abundance in spite of the risk.

Idrissa Simmonds

on blk girl magic, hip-hop, & other methods of sight

I feel most blk girl when I am surrounded by other blk girls, when I'm the only one for miles, when my mother reads my tarot, when the perm burns, when my coconut oil stains everything, when I worry about my brother getting pulled over by police, when Joycetta holds me in her prayers, when Grandmother Dear teaches me what she taught herself about money, when I wrap my hair in silk, when it's wash day, when it's Kujichagulia, when Aaliyah comes on, when I recite the lines to *A Preacher's Wife*, when my shed curls look like spiders out the corner of my eye.

I've spent a lot of time feeling not blk girl enough. I grew up in a historically Irish Catholic neighborhood attending mostly white schools during the week and a predominately Black Baptist church on Sundays. Our family celebrated Kwanzaa and Christmas, and our mother schooled us in the practices of Reiki and meditation. We had Erykah Badu & Stevie Wonder on the CD tower next to Alanis Morissette and Bruce Hornsby. This all felt natural to me until I left the microcosm of my family home and became introduced to the broader, segregated communities in my hometown of Chicago.

At church I was ashamed at the sharp syllables in my Easter Speeches, envied the lilt in my grandmother's voice. At school I hated the awkward hump the foam roller left in my permed bangs, wished my hair could flop effortlessly into a messy bun. Code switching was a mother tongue I could never really master. I wished I could navigate these seemingly disparate worlds with ease, to be multilingual in the ways these spaces seemed to demand. But some part of me always felt out of place. I stayed quiet a lot of the time, and it made me a good observer.

I learned the art of seeing from my grandmother. I was always impressed by the way she kept track of everything and everyone: Did you see that house on the corner went up for sale? You heard Mrs. Jackson's husband is sick? etc. My mother taught me there are ways of seeing beyond eyesight. Taught me to imagine white light around myself when entering new spaces that made me anxious. Taught me to read the signals in my gut, my intuition, messages that lay beneath the surface.

What first attracted me to hip-hop were the secrets, the allusions, the sampling. I loved the way the lyrics could be telling one story, and the layers of musical references in the production another at the same time. Hip-hop became a tool for me in my writing, to represent myself to myself. It gave me the language to articulate myself as a whole when I was so used to needing to leave parts of myself at the door in many situations. Hip-hop allowed me to make sense of my identity through collage—the juxtaposition and recontextualization of things that don't seem like they should make sense together, but somehow do.

Blk girl magic, to me, is a way of seeing for blk women in a world that often renders us invisible or misrepresents us in violent ways. It is the answer to my childhood worries of not fitting into a static notion of blk girlhood. It gives me permission to be expansive, to contain multitudes, to embrace contradictions and juxtaposition within myself and among my sisters.

This anthology is the second in a series of BreakBeat poetry anthologies, and represents a section of the cipher of Black womanhood. We are magic. Magic is a form of transformation, the way my sister lays my baby hairs with a toothbrush and a rat-tail comb, the way my grandmother makes family-sized melt-in-your-mouth peach cobbler for less than $10, the way my mother heals with her hands. My hope is that this anthology is a tool of transformation and illumination, so that we might always see ourselves as whole and evolving.

Jamila Woods

I shall become a
collector
of me
And put meat on my soul

—SONIA SANCHEZ

My Beauty

I found my beauty wearing a suit jacket
And I slapped her
Told her to love herself
And she put on a tie to spite me
My beauty found herself trapped in men's clothes
And it wasn't that I didn't look good
Just my beauty and I
didn't see eye to eye
Deep down we both knew that
as long as [we thought] I was a man
we would never be together
She feigned esteem
while I pointed out every flaw
She exerted a faux conceit
as I found more ways to hate myself
my stomach, my hair, my chest
I had always been arrogant
I had never known confidence
But I digress
My beauty kept trying
To make a man beautiful
dressing it in suits and sweaters
letting the stubble show some days
My beauty kept looking in the mirror
saying words like 'handsome' and 'sexy'
never believing them
I kept trying
To make my body a man
imagining it more muscular
calling broad shoulders masculine
I never saw my beauty

We kept looking past each other
in search of some boy
And ain't that being a Black woman
Being forced to destroy herself
To make a man more comfortable
Me and my beauty stopped looking for him one day
And suddenly
I saw my body
My beauty saw a woman
And me and my beauty
Finally saw each other
Finally saw this body
As the woman we've always been
Looked in the mirror and said,
"Hey girl"
And yeah, we cute.
We beautiful.

Rio Cortez

SELF PORTRAIT
IN A TANNING BED

It's February & I am the only black
girl at Future Tan Tanning
Salon I laugh when I enter
my private room & see an African
mask above the clothes racks I am
getting tired of irony naked
climbing onto the plexiglass &
hearing it creak I wonder like any
other moment alone what if I die
like this what if the plastic gives
& torched by two dozen ultra
violet glass rods I gently close
the canopy of the Suncapsule Super
Cyclone 350 wrapped in its purple
cylinders of light I can see myself
reflected back with tiny goggles at first
I think I look like a reverse coon with huge
black eyes but I like the way I look
darker & like a time-traveler how
my breasts must sometimes appear
like this to my lover I think I'm sad
or something worry how much time
has passed since I've been here

Texture

7

I wrap a towel around her shoulders.
Gently release the water from each strand

as if I were expressing the scent of a sachet
with every pass of the washcloth.

Tonight I am her lady in waiting.
Honored to guide the wide-toothed comb

from crown to nape and ear to ear
until her head is an aerial map of farmland

separated by oiled scalp roads. Once dripping
cotton. Now perfect plaits.

9

Barefoot in her Easter dress, my niece catches me
straightening my hair in my mother's bathroom.
In the mirror, she follows the reflection
of the infomercial steam iron, slowly raking
my fine frizzy curls into long silky strands
fit to sell for a fair price at a Chennai market.
she says, I want mine like that.

Before I can respond, she slides her body
between me and the countertop.
I clamp her hair between the iron plates,

steam rising with each pass. Erase
the crease the sponge roller left
while she slept the night before.
Every coiled puff on her head flattened stiff.

She admires herself, then runs to show
my mother and sister in the other room.
Fragments of our fallen tresses pepper
the white tile like feathers after a pillow fight.
I collect our black hair in a web of toilet paper.
Unplug the iron. Wash my hands.
Fasten my hair back into a ponytail.

11

At eleven
she looks about fourteen.
She wears waist length weaves
like the girls on Disney Channel.

The coarse hair at her temples
and kitchen broken
from constant brushing.
And flipping.

She begs to use my flat iron
because she doesn't know
synthetic fibers melt.
A slow burn.

13

I sent Ashley some pink pajamas with a sugar cookie motif for her
birthday. She's a full-on teenager now with a cropped punk haircut,

chipped nail polish, and a cell phone. The summer before last, she pulled the tangle of clip-in tracks from her head and tossed them on the deck as she splashed in the pool with her cousins. When I called them in for dinner, she ran a lap around the perimeter in her bikini. I think it was either an aqua blue or orange sherbet like the girl in Texas. Anyhow, she picked up speed, and right as her feet left the edge, she tucked her body into a perfect cannonball, then disappeared beneath the surface.

Mariahadessa Ekere Tallie

Homage to my Breasts (after Lucille Clifton)

these breasts are no longer stargazers
even alert they can't look a man
in the eye. they sighed milk
for two girl children who grew round
& learned the alphabet on pearls of mama dew,
these breasts became bread, then lowered
their dough heads, watched the children
crawl & walk. these breasts erased
memory of tongues craving
different food, two bowls of fire
cupped in a hungry man's hands.

This Body Keeps the Keys

My dear sparkly eyed polyps,
I don't have enough juice to
be the sole joist of this family
today

so I dream of clawfoot tubs
where I splash unapologetic
on how deep this umbilical gets
slumped from getting over,

hair unwashed, toenails randy
as hell because I am sincerely
mothered the fuck out, so tired
this mothering body

shellac lying facedown on a
coastline ashing & mottled
pockmarked canker sorrel
no good pictures of myself

skinbag workhorse bb creamery
constant upkeep of management
cultivation of self-care cosmetic
black pride goddess goddamn

this shit get tiresome putting so
much effort into what doesn't last
sometimes I want to retire shave
my head be a nun or a monk

just so I can forget all the years

time bludgeoned so I could look like
somebody else swimming around
in their own pallid wheel of tears

Yemaya, what is to become of us
I drag my body around lovingly but
it still won't let me go

You Mean You Don't Weep at the Nail Salon?

it's the being alone, i think, the emails but not voices. dominicans be funny, the way we love to touch—every greeting a cheek kiss, a shoulder clap, loud.

it gots to be my period, the bloating, the insurance commercial where the husband comes home after being deployed, the last of the gouda gone, the rejection letter, the acceptance letter, the empty inbox.

a dream, these days. to work at home is a privilege, i remind myself.

spend the whole fucking day flirting with screens. window, tv, computer, phone: eyes & eyes & eyes. the keys clicking, the ding of the microwave, the broadway soundtrack i share wine with in the evenings.

these are the answers, you feel me? & the impetus. the why. of when the manicurist holds my hand, making my nails a lilliputian abstract,

                    i close my fingers around hers, disrupting the polish, too tight i know then, too tight to hold a stranger, but she squeezes back & doesn't let go & so finally, i can.

Alysia Nicole Harris

WHITE GODIVA MELTS IN A MOUTHFUL OF BLOOD: PRAYER FOR MY UNBORN DAUGHTER

When I was young
the Southern boys asked me to open my legs
and I showed them a fountain
because what do teeth say against wood
or apple against dull kitchen knife?

My body already says the silence,
says the whiteness someone asked for
as a wedding present. I'm the lightest
peach on the tree.
When the child splits me
will she bare any of the taste?

Sometimes around family, I touch my belly, lower
my head. It's the guilt of bringing home a ghost.
It's everybody in the family praying for the ghost's light eyes.
It's Aaron's sperm making an alabaster baby inside my safest
blackest room and me, not knowing if there's enough
of Bennie Lee's blood in my veins to spill.

Every time he's on top of me, I mouth
Lover don't eclipse. A white shadow
is still a shadow that can cast,
and my mood is moon, as dark and as there
as a shadow, is a specter, is a haunting I never want to leave this bone house.

Shade may be shade but black ain't the same
invisible. I will not unpeel my darkness from her walls.
I want her born into this bruise.

Syreeta McFadden

ODE TO THE HYMEN

Index finger over pursed lips
We have no clue
how you separated yourself
landing here
on the floor of the shower
of my boyfriend's bathroom

My blood had come quickly this month
much to our surprise
our lovemaking was smoother
than it had been
And I
late for some student government thing
still slick with him
find you
curious piece of pitted peach
waiting

I cradle you in my palm
Call out to my lover and we examine
This lotus petal in the center of my palm
Water at my back
I extend my hand behind the shower curtain
As if this specimen is a puja
Flesh, still bright with red threads
And I'm like:

This is too big to be a hymen,
I thought it was a myth!

It's been years since

I could call myself
virgin
And I was late to the party
to embrace the trembling discoveries
of what my body could know
with another person
But seriously
This broken piece of tissue
must have shed herself from
a vagina larger than mine
Recently
We consider perhaps you
belonged to the couple next door
Whose loud thrashing had only minutes before
inspired our own need.

Pearlescent flesh
We pick at you lightly
With a child's curiosity, brushing you
like hairs on a caterpillar's back
In middle school
We split open clam shells
Dissecting mantle from exoskeleton
imagined ourselves surgeons
fingering the scalpel and pincer
to wrestle with the resistance till the
iridescent meat gave way
We were told sand collects there
Irritates the stomach
birthed pearls
Mystery could do such things

You suckerfish
Protector
The holiest of holies
There is no recorded description of the first temple
Vague imaginings of rituals

References to a small space where god will inhabit
They must have been praying to you
We do too
Arching our backs in unison
Rising to call your name
God's mouth
Revealing your face to the most worthy lover
You are Salome's first veil
dropped
You ripened fruit
Opening

my afropuffs

i got two moons / divided
by a rat tail comb
orbiting my good ideas
eclipsing the forehead
daddy gave

they said bad hair means
you look like a slave

but slaves made afro picks
outta scrap metal / hair
oil out of animal fat

*Slaves made
'bad hair' into
something beautiful*

grandma used to get us
permed once a month
60 dollars out her pocket
burning & forbidden to wash
itching & forbidden to scratch

what's more slave than that?

*? why do I
need to
conform?*

my afropuffs, shinin
made of glass, broke off
at the edges, sharp enough
to cut your fingers, soft enough
to be an impromptu pillow

hot to the touch, always sweating
oil from some fruit or nut, conducting
electricity clockwise, 3D printing
my signature over & over again
in new cursive

Morgan Parker

Magical Negro #217: Diana Ross Finishing a Rib in Alabama, 1990s

Since I thought I'd be dead
by now everything
I do is fucking perfect walking wreck
wreckless and men
I suck their bones until they're perfect
I don't sleep with accolades I don't get touched
in the night all men do is cry
and ask me to be their mammas I can't
get a decent fuck to save my
when I think about their feelings I don't care
It's cool it's cool come to mama there is so much
death here she is casual and almost fragrant like
the word kill doesn't sound as bad as it is
All my friends are sisters and husbands I'm afraid
to be uncharted I want an empire in my teeth but I can't
be bothered to not wear silk or nothing
I have grown up less mysterious than my myth
All men do is think I'm looking at them
When I think about them tasting me I don't
I mean don't google my tits when you can just
Unfortunately I have a body and I'm the only
one in charge of it you know what I eat the bones too
I'm in the world I'm in the world
nobody cares where I came from

why you cannot touch my hair

my hair is my childhood friend who used to come over every day and became cool in high school and then began to do drugs and then ran away but now is back trying to get her life together and we have coffee together one Sunday morning before her shift at the grocery store

my hair was in a zoo. my hair escaped from the zoo and took out three officers of the law before they shot my hair up full of tranquilizers. tranquilizers only because my hair is too valuable to die

my hair is a speakeasy. it's not that no one can get in—it's just that you don't know the password

my hair did a lot of work and climbed many mountains, literal and metaphorical, to get here. my hair ran out of oxygen tanks a mile back and has been heaving for breath ever since but is determined to reach the summit. my hair endured a bonnet last night. that's a lot of work

my hair is a technology from the future and will singe your fingertips, be careful

my hair doesn't care about what you want

my hair has a brother. I washed and conditioned and moisturized and combed and braided my hair's brother in the kitchen sink when my hair's brother was depressed. my hair's brother has a daughter. my hair's brother's daughter is tenderheaded and I sing while I comb her, holding her at the roots, touching her forehead so gently and telling her I love her while she cries

The first thing you do
is to forget
that I'm

Black.

Second,

you must never forget that

I'm Black.

—PAT PARKER

Bianca Lynne Spriggs

Big Black Bitch

after Mary Fields, aka "Stagecoach Mary"*

Ain't much a man can call me
I ain't already heard.
I stand taller 'n weigh more
'n even the legends say.
I pack two six-shooters
and a loaded ten-gauge
whether I sleep or ride.
And when shootin' don't work,
I pack these two fists.
I'm Black as a nightmare
to most of ya.
I'm Black.
My boots Black.
My coach 'n team Black.
And don't believe nobody
that say I ain't kept that den
of wolves at bay through
an entire Black night.
It was simple. They just needed convincin'
I was as bad or worse 'n any or alla them.
Don't matter whether you a dog,
a mule, or a man.
When I say *move*, I mean move.
And I don't need no whip

---

* Mary Fields was born a slave in Tennessee in 1832 and was the first Black woman to be employed as a mail carrier in the United States. She stood six feet tall and weighed over 200 pounds. She was known for smoking cigars, carrying pistols, drinking whiskey, and getting into the occasional fight with drunken cowboys.

like most of y'all white boys
to get my point across.
So what you ain't gon' do
is call me out my name
when I ain't in the mood.
And I ain't never in the mood
to be called outside a my name.
Fastest way to make me act my color.
I got this here run to make,
a reputation to uphold
for bein' on time,
'n the only thing standin'
'tween me, a pint of whiskey
and my end-a-the-day cigar is you.
And Neighbor, that ain't
a position I'd recommend.
So come on.
Call me that again.
So we can all find out what happens next.

Exile

Lorraine and I are sitting in her old apartment in the Village. Two Chicagoans in exile. She's smoking a black while I cradle a glass of Henny. Where can we go to be Black, Ms. Hansberry? The other side? Mars? I've been thinking about leaving. Is the only place for Black girls between the purgatory room and the edge of this universe? Lorraine takes a long drag and ashes her cigar.

Ode to Fetty Wap
(written after strip club)

A reading from the book of
Willie Maxwell 679:1738

. . . then Rap Gawd formed a man
from the dust of the auto tune
&breathed into his nostrils
the breath of Remy Martin,
the man became Fetty Wap.

Rap Gawd saw fit to
make Fetty a counterpart.
so he caused the man to fall into a deep sleep;
while he was sleeping,
he took one of the man's eyes
then closed up the place with flesh.
then the Rap Gawd made a woman
from the eye he had taken out of the man.

the creation story of Fetty,
the first trap rapper to make a song
I might play at my wedding.

there's a choir of church mothers
smiling down on the brown boy
that sings of a woman's worth
in a culture destined to nullify it.

do you know how long
sisters been waiting

for a brother
to willingly let us hit the bando?
(after patiently explaining what the fuck that means.)

l 'union fait la force
Your music emblematic of the motto of Haiti
unity makes strength

as we scream **SQUAAADDDD!**
the weight of that bass
hits hard
like Gawd's tears
landing on glow in the dark floors
'cause Gawd does not just "cry"
He makes it rain
on a crowd of women
in heels higher than most GPAs
dancing their way through
nursing school
&out of some deadbeat's
roach filled 1-bedroom.

the fellas
big brother
arm-wrapped shoulders
singing off key
about Ki's & pies
and other shit
they have no real idea about.

the only song in the club
that allows a hetero male
to gaze into the eyes
of another
[suspected] hetero male
and/or stranger
and sing his fucking heart out.

make him more mathematician
than murderer
spewing lyrics repping
the urban district's finest cognac
this,
is a black man's
Sweet Caroline
oh, oh, oh!

Fetty, you got me
I too see heaven
peering through
the pearly gated smile
of that gap toothed princess
in your video.

I too, have a glock in my rari;
in the form of a master's degree,
but don't get it twisted
this summa cum laude bloaw
any time a motherfucker think
they know me!
&my trap look a lot
like a dimly lit cafe
with semi-cold
red stripes
a microphone
a couple judges
but I'll be damned
if anyone tell me
I ain't a **queen of this shit.**

&then I blink
&the bass subsides
&the song fades
into another brother

caring more
about his golden grill
than making the best
of a family business.

&she picks up her ass,
her purse
slides off the pole
disappears
into a mixture
of low budget smoke machines
&catcalling men
wedding bands tangled
in the drawstring of their sweats

&another Saturday twerks itself into the crisp breeze of Sunday morning
&the church mothers glance over the room covered in government
issued confetti
&Gawd smiles
as they bellow in unison,

"I want you to be mine again"

At H&M, When Another Black Girl Asks If I Work Here

like my head wrap unfurled flagged
poached coast fashion motherland magazine
colored girl cover girl bent over nameless
offers and full page spread inside

poached coast fashion motherland magazine
mannequin dunked in chocolate pretzel posed
offers and full page spread inside
deboned battered chicken lard fried

mannequin dunked in chocolate pretzel posed
by a blur of brown hands knuckle cracked
deboned battered chicken lard fried
minimum wage manicure lickety spit shined

by a blur of brown hands knuckle cracked
the plastic hanger's cotton picked sweat dazzling
minimum wage manicure lickety spit shined
can I help you can I help you can I help

the plastic hanger's cotton picked sweat dazzling
snatching exactly *that* off the rack
can I help you can I help you can I help
these house nigga hips popping hard left right

snatching exactly *that* off the rack
movements razed-village economical
these house nigga hips popping hard left right
while speakers blast pop stick girls all white

movements razed-village economical
browsing through this bloodless coup
while speakers blast pop stick girls all white
guts of mama's gospel scooped out freeze dried

browsing through this bloodless coup
wallets fat with daddy's teeth
guts of mama's gospel scooped out freeze dried
tossed into baskets soul sore and tongueless

wallets fat with daddy's teeth
cavitied currency without a country
tossed into baskets soul sore and tongueless
ghost-heavy all-bruise body this Blackness

cavitied currency without a country
like my head wrap unfurled flagged
ghost-heavy all-bruise body this Blackness
colored girl cover girl bent over nameless

Cardi B Tells Me About Myself

Dear Frustrated in Flatbush,
Gurl, just go on ahead then.
You waiting for your Daddy
to give you the thumbs up?
Do what you like.
Do what makes your ass happy.
They gon call you all makes
and sizes of hoe anyway.
That's how this thing been set up.
But just cuz they name a thing, a thing,
Don't mean it ain't still named God
in some other language.

Your fortune cookie say you poppin.
You a full spread of good shit.
Your rotten wisdom tooth.
Your pockmarked shoulders.
Those eyelashes ain't come here
to talk about the weather.
You the hottest day in July
and every fire hydrant in this city
is written out to your name.

Whatchu dead fish for?
Whatchu call that stroke?
Drowning? Baptism?
Gurl, you betta lick that
collection plate clean
and stop pretending you just
got off the first canoe from Heaven.
You ain't nothin but

a big bowl of sweat rice.
You wring your left thigh
they call you Vintage JuJu.
They like, "This some kind of nightmare?"
And it's just you, smoking a blunt in the dark,
cackling like rain. Like your grandmama
at her ain't-shit husband's funeral.
Bitch, you been a woman.
This ain't new skin.
Slap some lycra on it
and call yourself a predicament.
You ain't just somebody's meal plan.
Pull back your hair and eat.

And look at this muhfukka,
sittin across the table,
lookin like he wanna bite you.
Tonight is tonight and tomorrow
might be somewhere else,
serenading some lesser bitch.
Throw his ass a bone and
stop worrying about your credit score.

You stay banging your tambourine
to the wrong hymnal.
I'm sure they had names
and inescapable mouths but
what your ex gotta do with this?
Why you still got his body in your linen closet?
That's nasty. Bitch, keep your house clean.
You crying over spilled dick. Gurl buh-bye.
Getchu a free refill.

You too black for indie film housewife.
You too naked for conversation like this.
Too much soft brutality,
too much bathtub depression.

Why you always got your neck swung open?
Free throat don't pay for your boy's sneakers.
You already know I don't even sigh for free.
Shit, I stroke a shallow strobe light,
inchworm down 4 feet of greasy pole,
and I still don't feel like any less than a miracle.

Syreeta McFadden

Question and Answer.
Or: Pirate Jenny Shit Talks
With Her Employer

And you see me kinda grinnin' while I'm scrubbin'
And you say, "What's she got to grin?"
I'll tell you.

There's a ship
The Black Freighter
With a skull on its masthead
Will be coming in!
—"Pirate Jenny" by Nina Simone

The black girl changed
her hair
Again.
Its angular and wiry spires
Twirl about her head
A nest of thorns, I think.
It's shorter than the last time I saw her.
So . . . I'm to assume she cut it?
The hair indicates sedition; I don't understand its appeal.
But I am curious.   How does she get it to stay that way?
How does it retain its sculptural form?
How does it not move when wind blows it?
What is it actually made of?
She considers my face in these questions.
Smiles, politely even, as she responds.
Her voice never wavers or breaks.
It has the quality of iron.
I taste pewter on my tongue.

She says:
It's made of 400 years of oppression from cracker bastards like you.
It's made of silkworm and cotton blossoms,
Milky Way dust.
It's your mother's first cell dividing into crystals,
Each strand is made of fractals.
Your whole soul's code,
Yours and mine,
            the embedded code of all humanity.
Human hair contains histories.
Here's mine: when I wash it shrinks to a sponge
Absorbs your bullshit questions
                    and your passive aggression.
Meaning, if you pull
it will resist.
My hair is switchblade: if you touch it,
you will bleed.
The black girl is made of salt and brine,
Mesquite and steel.
The black girl speaks like me
and it's here I discover
I crossed some sort of line?

Camonghne Felix

Meat

I turn off the Ferguson feed
and there is a Trader Joe's bag on
the table, my love hunched over a bowl beside
it, metal meeting mouth, a motion meant to nourish him.

I turn off the Ferguson feed
and there is this Trader Joe's bag on
the table & in the pinch of the trifold there is a
Pilgrim man holding a cylinder telescope but
I totally think it's a mullet, or a gun (if I'm going to
attend history, I might as well be accurate about it).

I turn off the Ferguson feed & sit quiet in my list
of generational traumas, reach for the man I want to marry
and pinch at the deep whiskey(d) skin for clarity—am I here?
Is he here? What is an existence under perpetual threat?

- A lisp
- A limited limb
- An identity of friction
- An identity of function

*

It's complicated when the self contradicts

It's complicated when I want my feminism
to serve everybody but that night a man slaps
the bold from my mouth, Soho's feminism
is a stiff frame choosing to mind its
own business

It's complicated when they're running
and dying and sitting in my classroom
and one of my seniors says "Miss
Camonghne, I don't give a fuck about
the cops," and I'm all sssssssh habibi,
end of the month quotas need filling

It's complicated when he says, "I'm just
trying to go to college so I don't have to
deal with this shit anymore," and I'm not
sure if it's better to leave him with the lie
or tug all the romance out of it

It's complicated when my star-eyed partner
says, "I couldn't do anything, babe, he had
me by the balls," about every dynamic in
which white men are present

       (always by the balls, always hanging from fucking something).

It's complicated when he says "this is
chess, babe" and I just want to know
what happens when we move

                  *

White girl says,
"when they stare or say things to me on the street, it makes me
    uncomfortable, it makes
                        me feel like a piece of meat,"

A piece of meat gets shot in the face on a doorstep while seeking help after
    a car accident.

A piece of meat is shot 11 times on a residential street corner.

A piece of meat is rolled up dead, left to expire in a gym mat,

A piece of meat is shot blind in the middle of the night.

The dead pieces of meat are left to slow bleed on public platforms, like a tree or highways and street corners.

This is how the butchers' display their prime cuts with pride.

A piece of meat is anxious in a Greenpoint grocery store.

Pieces of meat fight over how to respond to being pieces of meat in this Greenpoint
grocery store. The pieces of meat deliberately move faster, the pieces of meat deliberately move slower, the butcher stands by, clean knife to be deployed, two flies and a honey trap before midnight.

*

I turn off the Ferguson feed and there is a Trader Joe's
bag on the table. In the pinch of the trifold
there is a white man holding
a gun (if I'm going to attend history
I might as well be accurate
about it).

Britteney Black Rose Kapri

micro

actually i don't understand martha, what do you mean when you say i speak so well? Oh, where did you expect me to work mary-beth? i don't remember saying i lived on the South Side muriel. are you telling me your hair doesn't grow 30 inches overnight melanie? if i'm not like the other ones, then who am i like melissa? do you follow everyone around the store macy? when you say my sentences connect do you mean like a conjunction molly? well, where else could I have gotten my degree myrtle? maggie, i don't think i understand what you mean by urban? are all kids inner city youth or just the Black ones marilyn? so . . . missy, beyoncé is your spirit animal . . . explain. and why wouldn't you go back after you go Black mallory? let me clarify when you say you wish you had skin like mine do you mean scarred or sensitive maureen? do they not have chicken where you're from magda? mckenzie, what's your name mean . . . no I mean back where your family's from? i don't think I can be racist, i have a white friend miranda, right?

I do not weep at the world—I am too busy sharpening my oyster knife.

—ZORA NEALE HURSTON

Idrissa Simmonds

Kingston, Jamaica. 3am.
Passa Passa Dance Party.

One good thing about music/when it hits/you feel no pain
—**Bob Marley, Trenchtown Rock**

When her body is a compass
bearing South, and she is crouched
bare-toed and feckless above steaming pavement
poised to give birth to drum or bass,
Red Bull triggered at the wrist,
hips a bouquet of cackling fingers,
lips two hummingbirds aimed for flight,
the Glock-Nined baby brother
she nursed from croup
with lavender oil and Cat's Claw bark,
for whom she turned a fist of nothing
into school fees and uniforms,
and whom she will bury
in St Andrew Parish Church Cemetery
once the sun fully rises,
feels more like a brilliant toothache
her tongue worries,
than a tumid and wild devastation.

Outside my Harlem Window

On the brick red stoop of the brownstone next door
is a steady rock black man sellin harps to the neighbors
by blowin a blues riff like it's nobody's business.
Except it is: his, to remind us the potential
impromptu music on a Tuesday, on top of Sugar Hill
has to make you wanna wear your church shoes
and creased slacks for no reason other than to give up joy.

This man, with two hands full of harp, havin church
on the stoop of the brownstone next door, is, with his right hand,
blowin this—which he call Black Magic—slow
into a soprano note on the far side of the harp first,
sliding low as he can go, then, catching each and every note
in between and ridin high the riff back again to the peak
which pierce clean, like the call of some sacred steel winged black bird.

Ain't no fear filled trill on this stoop. Not this Tuesday.
Not this Harlem broke open early like popping into
an August bell pepper with your fingers,
and all the seed and fruit inside of you is exposed now
and yellow or green and red and black, magic
and he is wide nosed, and he is pinky ringed.
He is my grandfather, this man.

Old timin swag and all, grey, leaning over the back
of a barbershop chair saying something of how the sunsets
in the South come in colors you ain't never seen, like the rural red
on an Alabama backyard, the white peach pink of a cuticle
peeled back to the flesh from pullin cotton from the hull. And
sometimes, he'll push his left hand out to show you exactly where.

And sometimes he'll get to jingling the coins in his pocket.
And sometimes he'll get to leanin on his back leg, poke
his breast out, pull a harp from his chest pocket and get to blowin
like a yellow headed blackbird, all his unrest and scar and laughter
building its own back beat on a blues harp for 3,000 people
at a Tuskegee jubilee. He is 4H, hog raisin, harp blowin, handsome.
And somehow you know your granddad is James Cotton,
is Junior Wells, broke and black as Alabama ever and trouble, "man,

y'all don't even hear me!" he'll stop to say.
But I do hear you granddad. All the way out here
in Harlem, where the steady rock black man
make a mimic of you, sellin old spice and wisdom,
holding church on a Tuesday, on a stoop
for the other men who gather, double park,
unroll their windows, unfurl for a minute.

Listen: if he didn't have his other hand full
of wanting, of his wonted work to sell,
he would put both hands on his harp
smile his lips over the harp,
he would lean back like my granddad,
like an old tree, let the wind blow through him
and make a miraculous and joyful noise.

A Brief History of Coconut Oil

You want to know what God I pray to/ I pray to whatever
God that could best moisten the coil of my hair/ There is a
myth that states brown women have fountains levitating
above our skulls/ We walk with our palms stretched out
Gold and humming/ Ready to lead a choked desert to
salvation/ All of our hair brittle and died when the state forgot
our great, great nana's last name/ All of the water within us
fled to refill the ink missing from their birth certificates/ If
you cannot pinpoint your name on a piece of paper then you
do not exist/ So our fountains cracked and withered/ Its
marble fell into our scalps like sharp snow/ Our blood was
not wet enough to moisten the rubble/ So we prayed for rain
but instead received oil/ Made due with the scraped intestines
of a bronze fruit/ Who sang a song that was the same color
as our skin

Ariana Brown

Black Girl Magic

Supremacy

i want to talk about white women.
i want to talk about fifth grade &
dominic jackson garcia, the afrolatino
boy whose holy mouth chose the white
girl instead. as a girl, i had a slew
of white best friends. black boys
shared hot cheetos with me, held
hands with them, more concerned
with aspen & kaedee than my glossy
neck. they wanted to swallow a white
girl's smile, fold it in their pockets
to keep them warm. i, frozen on the black-
top, redhanded embarrassment. i'm ready to talk
about white women. how the lyft driver,
black man, blames his black girlfriend
for his inability to pay rent. how he breaks
open his saliva to drown my body, says,
"i'm just gonna get me a white woman.
no offense." i want to talk about white
women. the ones who step in front of me
in line, who follow me in stores, who
grab my hair shoulders arm
whatagreattattooivealwayswantedadreamcatcher
iloveyourhairhowdidyougetitlikethat
imtouchingyoutoproveimnotuncomfortable
i want to talk about white supremacy.
supreme, meaning *superior to all others.*
as in, diana ross and the supremes.
as in, moonwalk so supreme make yours
look earthly. i'm extraterrestrial.
got two moons for feet & heaven

say my name a galaxy. is this
what you meant when you said
i'm too angry? too sure about
the limits of this world, that i
spoke about pain like a thousand
sharecropping grandmothers, that
i exaggerated, that i wasn't nice
the way white women make you feel?
supreme, meaning *strongest, most important,*
or most powerful. so i flash my teeth,
catch light in my mouth. grow my
hair thick as a plague. don't speak
when i'm speaking. white men apologize
to me now. men of color call me difficult.
i roll my eyes, hold my heart like the
gift it is, hold the hearts of my sisters.
supreme, meaning *involving death.*
as in, supreme sacrifice. black women
everywhere you thought we weren't—
germany holocaust mexico conquest
slavery global economy—
the worldwide girlchildren of empire.
they ain't got numbers bold enough
to count the ones we've lost. supreme,
last definition: *a rich cream sauce.*
my mother buys sauce packets for
17 cents at the grocery. says, they're
no good for you. says, they're all salt.
they're all lot & his wife, city on fire:
rosewood: burning because of a white
women's expression. the hair like
woven silk, skin color of whole milk,
crosses my path like an ancient warning.
in what version of the story do black
women win?

Rio Cortez

THE END OF EATING EVERYTHING

after Wangechi Mutu

I toss my colossal head back and let it roll
open my wide mouth, it is glossed up & pussy
pink my face is a magazine in cuts like I said
I open my mouth after hunting and eat up
all the birds whole bird tribes, I enter
their murmuration and exit hemorrhage
it's whatever at first I look like a pretty girl
& then you see the giantess I've been I've eaten
everything I have kept no pet to love
my eyelids goldmelt I use my face to get
a little closer how the coyote changes its howl
at the canyon mouth and toward them come sweet
pups my belly lined with wooly afghans
from my grandmother's house and yours
even the front porch I've eaten I am nothing
but exhaust now I am puckered up and black
smoke rising I smile and anything surrenders
this enormous don't they see me coming

SARA BAARTMAN AND I
NEGOTIATE VISIBILITY

I hate to fold in public, but Sara insists that the fabrics stay pressed longer if you set the creases fresh out the dryer. Side-by-side at this laundromat, our hips brush while we arrange our clothes. We fold our panties differently. Hers in two, like closing a silk book; mine in a tri-fold. A man behind us snickers and I turn. His phallus is exposed through the open mouth of his zipper. I am reminded of a premature eggplant still umbilicaled, condensed in color, more night sky than mature purple. He looks at both of us and back down at his produce. I hate to fold in public. Sara turns too and laughs. She walks up to him. For a moment I wince thinking of his flesh caught in those metal teeth, but she reaches down the front of her own shirt. He looks at me while she chases something she's hidden between her breasts. A single dollarbill falls out and onto the grey tiled floor. For the show, she says, before returning to me and teasing a hug out from under my crossed arms.

Syreeta McFadden

OF THEE, MAGICAL NEGROES, I SING

(or: Film Stills from a Future Oscar-Award-Winner Featuring a Black Girl Archetype)

1.

Lula Perry, I'm told, only wore red lipstick. Cherry red lipstick. She was a high, high yellow, very fashionable lady among the colored folks in a black white world. And in this world, the year would be 1952, Jackson, Tennessee. She'd scoop up Barbara, then 8 years old, knocked kneed and ashy legged, for adventures outside my then grandma Mary Sue's house. In those days, you didn't let a child wander off on her own and Lula, high yellow and cherry red lips, white girl framed with negro child in tow, would pack two lunch boxes; a snack for ashy kneed, bright-eyed Barbara and treat for them white folks. Cause that's how everyone spoke of them then, *them white folks*. On the white side of town in Jackson, Lula Perry was sophisticated enough to walk among beasts.

The other lunch box contained an assortment of colorful gift bags I imagine. With doilies, maybe dusted with tea rose or honeysuckle powder. They must have been delightful little bags, tempting enough to prompt white folks to accept them from one of their seeming own. Pretty little bags, filled with feces. Lula Perry, I imagine from this story must have been out of her ever loving mind to risk her body and that of 8 year old ashy kneed Barbara, now 67 year old Barbara who is now telling me this story in hushed tones that one would use passing on family secrets. We're sitting on a bench at the berth of the Staten Island Ferry. It is September in New York. 2011. That shit is cray cray. Crazy. In my memory of things I've never witnessed, I imagine the face of Dorcas, that woman that drove Violet so mad, she'd cut up the face of a dead girl. Lula had to be that kind of beautiful. Mad woman. Barbara says they'd sit on a park bench far enough out of sight to watch them white folks open up their "gifts," twist their faces up, appalled. I imagine them reaching in the bag thinking it a chocolate, bringing it close to the lips, biting, smearing shit around stiff white collars pressed by black wrinkled worn hands, balled fists when the crease was off just so, when that fucker called her nigger. Lula would never clean anybody's home. She skewed too far white and here is where I know that in the fall of my sophomore year in college, when I would trip white folks for no reason other than I could, that Lula must have been traveling with me.

2.

In this black and white world of 1952 a grandmother I never knew, except in the sepia stained portrait that hung in my grandmother's home, her body began to pearl with tumors. And somewhere just a little north and east, an indigo stained glass sample would be cradled in white hands in white gloves in a white lab. And this woman's body too would be pearled by tumors and cysts. Both would die in this black and white world. But the indigo stained cells would thrive.

3.

Caroline. Hoke. Corrina. Corrina. Minny. Bagger Vance. John Coffey. Uncle Remus. Jim. Jesus. Barack Obama. Esu Elegba. Herman Cain. Michael Steele. Lula. Mary Sue. Henrietta. Harriet. Lucy. Saartjie. Phyllis. Michelle. Mahogany. Erykah. Beyoncé. Cleopatra. Dido. Josephine. Dorothy. Madea.

4.

White babies love me. Let me be specific: little white blond blue-eyed baby boys in strollers love me. It's my hair. I get it. Spongy and squishy. I tell their mothers they'll fall in love with a girl just like me someday. I tell this to a mother who just bought a copy of *The Help*. I say, "that's the kind of power these almond shaped eyes have."

5.

When I was in high school, Granny once told me her theory behind the adage the *blacker the berry, the sweeter the juice*, and alternatively its cousin, *once you go black, you don't go back*.

The vagina.

She postulated that white men believe that black cooters possess some super secret sexy mojo. She said that this is what they tell each other about girls that look like me. She said this to me after Jack, who was white, dropped me home after play practice.

6.

Last night at dinner with a mutual friend of a friend—the details of the relations really don't matter so much as the discussion—which centered on a harrowing recounting of the March from Selma to Montgomery. Someone, let's say, a Negro, sighed deep into the meniscus of his red wine glass mumbling only so audible, "if every white person was on that bridge in Selma, surely it woulda collapsed."

I'm sitting next to him. These are the mysterious exchanges we have in mixed company.

7.

The sheer logistics and painstaking, determined focus to prepare gift bags of shit to leave on the white side of town in 1952 Jackson, Tennessee, let's concentrate on these facts for a moment, shall we?

8.

For this part, I will borrow the voice of Morgan Freeman:

Lula Perry's heartbreak probably begins at the hands of a white man. Then doubled by the hands of a black man. At this point, Lula fair skinned, cherry red lip, sought solace from the blacker women in her family. Those women, likely dismissive of this golden child, who was able to move between black and white worlds with relative ease, Lula is reminded of the verse where the cock crowed three times and Peter denies knowing Jesus before he was brought to slaughter, and those Perry girls, they were dark solid stock. And Lula remembers pretending not to see Mary Sue on Main Street in the noonday sun.

Packing gift bags of shit for them white folks had to have been some kind of penance. Do this in the remembrance of me, Lula muttered to herself in the kitchen.

The year was 1952. Henrietta Lacks and Mary Sue Perry-Crymes would never meet. And Henrietta, some sixty years later, long after her bones settled into chalk dust, would become famous. Indirectly, like Lucy's bones in Africa, the cradle of civilization, Henrietta too would contain the key to life in that bitter death. And her cells will multiply.

9.

Twenty years ago, I tripped white people for two straight months. It was magical. They apologized to *me*. I recognized the irrationality behind this experiment. But particulars emerged: eyes and breath. Their eyes always said shock, fear. I am a small-framed woman, and in our contrived collision, our bodies knocked together in an unwelcome tumble. They were supplicant, terrified. Their breath would draw in deep then release a gasp or quiver.

They owed me nothing. They owed me everything.

Magical Negro #607: Gladys Knight on the 200th Episode of *The Jeffersons*

Privilege is asking other people
to look at you. I like everything
in my apartment except me.
I mean I need to buy a toaster.
What is the point of something
that only does one thing.
My life is a kind of reality.
When I get bored, I close the window.
By the way what is a yuppie.
Here I am, two landscapes.
My tattoo artist says I'm a warrior
with pain. I tell her we can manifest
this new moon in six months.
When I'm rich I will still be Black.
You can't take the girl out of the ghetto
ever. It's too much to ask to be
satisfied. Of course I sing
through the struggle. My problem is
I'm too glamorous to be seen.
How will I know when I've made it.
In the mirror will I have a face.
How long does a good thing last.
Sometimes eating a guilty salad
I become a wife.
Let me be the woman

who takes care of you.
Weezy and George in drapes
and crystal silverware.
By the way predominantly white
means white. I want to be the first
Black woman to live her life
exclusively from the bathtub.
Making toast, enjoying success
despite my cultural and systemic
setbacks. I was raised to be
a nigger you can trust.
I was raised to be better
than my parents. In a small house
with a swamp cooler
I touched myself. I wanted to be
in the white mom's carpool.
My cheek against something new
and clean. I clean my apartment
when I am afraid of being
the only noise.
Everyone I know is a Black man.
Me I'm a Black man too.
Tragically, I win. It is a joke.
I always require explanation:
Life, Dope. I am so lucky to be you.
When something dies,
I buy a new one.

Britteney Black Rose Kapri

for Colored boys who considered gangbanging when being Black was too much

i saw / three little black boys / lying in the grave yard / i couldn't tell / if they were playing / or practicing.
—**Baba Lukata**

like all Black Chicago women i
have been preparing my womb to carry a stillborn.
a baby to grow, but not man. i
will bury him before i have finished
paying off his first hospital bills. i
have picked my daughter's name.
but can't bring myself to ready the words i'll
need for his tombstone. i
am trying to line my womb with Kevlar.
like all Black Chicago women I
have been preparing my womb
to carry a Bigger Thomas,

my son is a name no one knows
in homicide tracker. or a blurb
in the tribune. a clutched purse, a whistle
in the wrong direction. a Black boy drowning.
There is no ticking, just the cock of the hammer banging against my
biological clock waiting for me to offer a new sacrifice to these streets

what I mean when I say
I'm sharpening my oyster knife

I mean I'm here
to eat up all the ocean you thought was yours.
I mean I brought my own quarter of a lemon,
tart and full of seeds. I mean I'm a tart.
I'm a bad seed. I'm a red-handled thing
and if you move your eyes from me
I'll cut the tender place where your fingers meet.

I mean I never met a dish of horseradish I didn't like.
I mean you're a twisted and ugly root
and I'm the pungent, stinging firmness inside.
I mean I look so good in this hat
with a feather
and I'm a feather
and I'm the heaviest featherweight you know.
I mean you can't spell anything I talk about
with that sorry alphabet you have left over from yesterday.

I mean
when I see something dull and uneven,
barnacled and ruined,
I know how to get to its iridescent everything.
I mean I eat them alive.

what I mean is I'll eat you alive,
slipping the blade in sideways, cutting nothing
because the space was always there.

"No, I do not weep at the world—I am too busy sharpening my oyster knife."
—Zora Neale Hurston

It is our

duty to
fight

for our freedom.

It is our duty to win.

We must love each other
and support each other.
We have nothing to lose
but our chains.

—ASSATA SHAKUR

Ariana Brown

A Brief Life

so i'm wearing a black lives matter hoodie &
walking through campus / because the protest
is in a few minutes & the joke is / i'm wearing
black on black & standing near the jefferson davis
statue / i mean i'm standing near the stump
where the jefferson davis statue used to be / he
was removed formally a few months ago / now
only his name remains / engraved / in stone / &
the joke is i'm wearing a black lives matter hoodie
standing next to the ghost of jefferson davis &
of course / the campus police are driving by
at this exact moment / & i turn away / as though
black isn't a vacuum of light / a gap left by loss
a space entirely devoid of matter / a glitch in
the sunlight / as though the police will not
detect the ghosts they left me with / as though
i'm not always wearing blood on blood / &
because of the ghosts / or the heat / or their own
preference for intimidation / the police keep
driving / i take the back way to reach the protest
anyway / the protest / which isn't even that large
which is being monitored by police / & i take a paper
with the chants / & the joke is there's at least ten chants
& that's a lot to remember / for someone who was late
to the protest / & walked past the ghosts of slave
patrollers / & we begin marching / & white students
in collars are laughing / & i am offering my lungs to
the hungry spirit among us / trying to hear the chants
in the back of the procession / to make sure we are
chanting the same thing / in the front / & we are moving
through the campus streets / & cars are honking / & when

we reach guadalupe street / the city bus drivers / all black
& tired / are waving / snapping / hollering / hallelujahing
out the windows / & we are not met with tools of violence
& i don't know what to make of that / & this is not
my first protest / but this is the first protest / in which my
grief did not become me / instead / my body leaned
toward my roommate / who organized the thing / &
looking over / i watch her / dance / arms wound
in freedom / a good gospel / releasing from her limbs
& she smiles at me / & i join / & the chanting is loud
& immoveable / & nobody dies on the street / &
the ghosts pull this brief life from their palms / &
place it in mine / & the joke is one time
i went to a protest / wearing a black lives matter hoodie
& i danced with my roommate / knowing full well
i was hated / & knowing full well
i was loved

Aja Monet

#SayHerName

i am a woman carrying other women in my mouth
behold a sister, a daughter, a mother, dear friend.
spirits demystified in a comrade's tone. they gather
to breathe and exhale, a dance with death we know
is not the end. all these nameless bodies haunted

by pellet wounds in their chest. listen for us in
the saying of a name you cannot pronounce, *black*
and *woman*, is a sort of magic you cannot hashtag.
the mere weight of it, too vast to be held. we hold
ourselves, an inheritance felt between the hips

woman of soft darkness. portal of light, watch them
envy the revolution of our movement. we break
open to give life flow. why the terror of our tears,
torment of our taste. my rage is righteous. my love
is righteous. my name is righteous. hear what i am

not here to say, we, too, have died. we know we are
dying, *too*. i am not here to say, look at me, how i
died so brutal a death, i deserve a name to fit all
the horror in. i am here to tell you, how if they
mention me in their protests and their rallies,

they would have to face their role in it, *too*, my
beauty, *too*. i died many times before the blow
to the body. i have bled many months before
bullet to the flesh. we know the body is not the
end. call it what you will but for all the hands,

cuffed wrists of us, shackled ankles of us, the

bend over to make room for you of us, how dare
we speak anything less than *i love you*. we who
love just as loudly in the thunderous rain as when
the sun shines golden on our skin and the world

kissed us unapologetically. we be so beautiful
when we be. how you gon be free without me?
your freedom tied up with mine at the nappy
edge of our soul singing with all our sisters. watch
them stretch their arms in my voice, how they
fly open-chested toward your ear, listen for

Rekia Boyd
                                        Tanisha Anderson
            Yvette Smith
                            Aiyana Jones
Kayla Moore
                                Shelly Frey
Miriam Carey
                        Kendra James
            Alberta Spruill
                                    Tarika Wilson
                    Shereese Francis
                                    Shantel Davis
            Malissa Williams
                                            Darnisha Harris
Michelle Cusseaux
                            Pearlie Golden
                                                    Kathryn Johnston
                        Eleanor Bumpurs
            Natasha McKenna
                                        Sheneque Proctor
                    Sandra Bland

                                        we are each saying,

we do not vanish in the bated breath of

our brothers. show me, show me a man
willing to fight beside me, my hand in his,
the color of courage. there is no mountaintop
worth seeing without us. meet me

in the trenches, where we lay
our bodies down
in the valley
of a voice

         say it   say   her   name.

Purgatory Room

It's me, Sandra and Rekia in the back of the purgatory room. I snuck in
  a bag of
Vitner's Crunchy Kurls and now our fingertips are covered in a dusty film
  of red.
Rekia say she don't remember the last time she's shot the shit like this.
  Everything is
fuzzy and her ears still ring from the buckshot. Sandra say this is the first
  fun she's had
in this place.

Venessa Marco

Patriarchy

The man behind the bodega counter
asked me if I could deep throat

Said,

"you look like the kind of girl who can swallow,
who can make a man forget that his girl doesn't do certain things"

In an attempt to respond
I thought,

Irrational of me,
to be both woman and hungry

to confuse myself with the kind of person who has rights

to be woman and house a body
is to break all the floors
is to know most men think your mouth a door
think your mouth; always open
think you, stedfast ready
think you beckon their call
their call loud as sirens
their sirens break all the windows
you, woman, house a body, that stay breaking
creaking men, think the fragments are an opening
walk through you like your walls are an invitation
run their fingers through all your panels
you don't recall thinking yourself a welcome mat
except for the fact that you came out the womb
both woman and body

and men like most people want to crawl back into that body
and you, woman, are a body that both absorbs and expels

So naturally, you the first they coming for

dare speak?

bitchfeminist
man basher, even though you ain't bashing all men,
just the men who treat women and think this kind of way
Still you're
manhater,
You be mad lonely,

Ain't no man gonna love you
echo loudly

Like, that's the only accomplishment
Us women strive for
Like, that's the only role us women play

Patriarchy so evident
it seeps through every floor you got
until everyone is calling you out your name
you, no longer stacy
you, whore from downtown
head game so good
gotta man walking in the right direction
see, how quickly, you become a mouth again?
a cavity
half temple and brothel
both cathedral and jezebel
cattle and disparaged
you, are not just dressed up
high heels stomping pavement
you, you asking for it

as if your body
were an eager child who can't use its words

you, woman, can't form words but movement
movement demands attention
attention says you deserve everything you get

Regardless if you wanted it

Because, what do you know of desire
Except for what is told to you

What do you know of your body
Except for what is told to you?

Who are you except for what is needed from you?

What is needed from you other than a mouth and the right kind of
softness?

So, I stood there
My jaw a waving flag
Legs the right kind of run ready
and said,

If your girl can't swallow
How does she eat?

All The Things That Have Not Happened Between Us

How come the same guy gets head in every poem?
He's white, from the suburbs. If he's young, his parents are away.
If he's older, he's an artist who uses industrial materials to create
what the speaker, in all her blonde, bobbed feminism
calls "beauty." The tip is always pink, the balls
"smell like sex." Sometimes, semen gets in her hair;
sometimes he drools, or curses at her, and the spittle
dribbles into his beard. He likes to hump her mouth while playing
with her breasts, and I can never figure out the logistics—
are his arms really long? And black women rarely give head
in poems. Perhaps for the same reason a black woman
won't give head in this one.   But I'd like to.
I imagine you're gentle, and I know I'm talking about
your dick, but I can't think of anything more political to say.
Black love is a lot like other loves—that is, beneath
the conversations we have about death.
The way our bodies vanish, how sometimes
I want to vanish into someone safer, saner,
more whole than me. But the greatest heartbreak
is when you realize the one you love can't protect you, might
live to hate you for it. Might shove your face
into his crotch because it makes him feel—I don't know.
Hasn't that already been said? I'm trying to find the right way
to say "you." I was going to begin with: "It was April,
in her salmon-colored wet" because I wanted
to describe the day of our first text, but seriously:
"salmon-colored"? I'm talking about pussy, though I'm not sure
our parts should ever meet. That, I suppose, is the best thing
about us—what's left: you, blood-filled, unmapped
in your distant house. The glorious first touch of you.
Everything else.

Kemi Alabi

Mr. Hotep Says #Blacklivesmatter and He'd Kill a Dyke

The dyke within
tires of
the nigger without,

sick of rope
when the brick
calls her name.

Same blood,
same alley,

wrong hands,
wrong headline,

wrong barking pack
circling the same
hellmouth,

same body
split, cracked
open.

Wrong balm
slicked
on the sin,

wrong North

guiding the killer's
new heart,

wrong village
tasked
with forgiveness,

same torches
blackening
the door.

All the women
in this body
burn at once,

no matter
how wrong
the fire,

& oh god,
the sound:
a chorus,

the notes,
softer
in sum,

a dirge
for killer's
hands

as they
surely break
bread

for a lover
with half

this face

and twice
the room
for flame.

rememory

My body soft

fresh milled cotton.
A deep brown of dried
blood stain.

> stumblin'
> into
> the spots
> blood spilled into my
> internet. Look
>
> up on the
> train, I'm in
> Fruitvale.
> Can hear the protest of asphalt
> that know it ain't
> made for mausoleum.
>
> In Brooklyn, I follow
> Cousin up dark
> "Pink Houses" stairway.
> Grab my chest,
> try to catch Akai's
> last breath. Cousin
> already at the door,
> ain't look back
> or think twice. This
> where she live.

Here
I am, blood
blackened girl.
All up in other
niggas memories
on accident.

If I cried every time
I stood where some
body colored like
mine lost life
I don't think I'd be soft

no more. Think I'd dry up.

No time

for the little
joy I find pressed
up against a body
that ain't dead
yet.

Just salted fault lines
down my face,
cracks in the fullness
of my lips

And what then
will they call me

but dirt.

Mahogany L. Browne

If 2017 Was a Poem Title

1.

When they turn bodegas into boutique grocery stores
When they bounce cops up the block
Like this hipster protection program won't turn back
Lefrak into Harlem turn back Harlem into Chirac
turn back BedStuy into Brownsville turn Brownsville back
Into the Bronx back into Gaza back . . .

You will taste this strange and bitter American history

Where the Mom and Pop work more hours than the Governor
Where the pesticides overflow our sewer systems
Float our food deserts into neighborhoods
One way in
One way out
Tell me this gentrification be for my own good
Tell me this housing project keep us warfare ready
Tell me Biggie died for our sins
& I'll show you a Brooklyn stoop with a babies' name etched in chalk
A hashtag ghost gone already
A price tag on his sister's face
She's been missing since Sunday
Where choppa lights paint concrete a trail of breadcrumbs
A haunting finding its way back to our homes

1.

    The Electoral College is
    a lullaby designed to put us
    back to sleep.

1.

The ocean is weeping a righteous rage, she got questions for the living:
& what about the sweetheart who would grow to love Tamir Rice? Mike
    Brown? Korryn Gaines? Akai Gurley? What about they mamas singing
    their name before each breakfast?
Or the church praying for their redemption—bibles raised in the air?
What about their (almost) children? How about they Daddy's smile?
What about they name make them so easy to turn to ash?
How we ghosting Black boys for the toys we gift them?

1.

On a Monday
A white body told my Black body
It ain't earned no apology for the bloodshed
For the nights when my skin grow so cold
I know I must be inches from death
For each death hand-delivered to me,
              this: silence   this: certain dismissal   this: post racial reality
    show   this: confederate hug
& don't it bloom like a mushroom sky?
What about the blues? Why it cry like hail? Why it hell like America so
    so long

1.

Yo: America

Whatchu know about noose ready
Whatchu know about chalk lines & double barrels
Whatchu know about a murder weapon
Or a loose cigarette
Or a baby sleeping on a couch

Whatchu know about the flag
The confederate fathers
The truck that followed me down a lonely road in Georgia
The names that I rolled off my tongue in prayer?

Saint Sojourner
Saint Harriet
Saint Rekia
Saint Sandra

Bring me home

Or leave me steady
Gun aimed and cocked ready

Con artist turned 45th resident of the White House
While the 44th President is lifted off the grounds
              by his shadow & his Black wife
She sideeye all day
She cheekbone slay

While the media aim and shot at his presidential legacy
Until weed smoke & a concert make us remember BLK people ain't never
    been human here

Ain't we beautiful, those that survived the purging
Those that spill, body splay beautiful from a hateful song
This swing sweet sweet low spiritual ain't neva been inclusive

Whatch know about larynx & baton
How you sing him crow in the key of Emmett Till
What fever fuss you awake?
Who else got cop'd anxiety?
Call it what it is: Post traumatic slave syndrome
Call it land tax until homeless
Call it abortion turned sterilization
Ain't no lie like the one against our stillborn children
Ain't no lie like the many that shaped our babies into mute cattle
Prison industrial complex reverberates in the tune of elementary
              4th graders are the easiest targets

1.

A Math Problem:
If 1 woman, got a 7 Mac 11
& 2 heaters for the beemer
How many Congress seats will the NRA lose?
How many votes will it take for a sexual predator
    to lift the White House off her feet?

1.

I am practicing this aim
This tongue a shoestring strafe
My tongue say:

  Melt the wires of Guantanamo
  Yasin Bey coming home ain't what we thought it would be
  Ain't no solace in Mecca
  Even Spike Lee left Brooklyn
  Here, a slumlord will leave my front steps
  Full of rat piss & AirBnB my neighbors' apartment
    for half my take home pay
  Unhinge the city of Rikers
  Bring back the reapers
  Give them the loot & the stoop

Yea, they good at killin' but so was Jefferson.
I mean Washington. I mean CIA. I mean Cointelpro.
I mean they mimic your Grace. I mean it's a 2017, America.
A new new year & your facelift be botched.

Magical Negro #80: Brooklyn

Here is the bright, young food co-op.
Here is the steeple. Here are the royals
not yet dead. Here are the Niggas With
Amethyst crystals. Shea butter
halos orbit half-shaved heads bowed
for vindication. Our mother patchouli
who art in the apothecary on Flatbush
hallowed be your Dutch wax dress.
Give us this day we light soy candles
for dead brothers. Give us this day we soak
our supremacy wounds.
Give us this day.
Give us fresh juice green
as avocados, and strength
to dismantle Fox News. We are marching
even in our sleep. We are reading
Du Bois, getting high off the salt eaters.
Thy kingdom come to yoga. Thy will
be a black feminist Tumblr. Thy will is not
our struggle. Forgive us. We have gathered
to learn to pronounce *freedom*.
Procession body roll, communion oysters
with prosecco. Roses for our waist beads.
We have moved away from suburbia.
Now we live on Saturn.
We don't pray anymore
the way our parents taught us.
Instead we stack our arms
with wood and music
hatches from our tongue rings.
Hymns for the dead, hookahs for

the almost-dead. Praise our half-lives.
Our bodies break but we still sage them.
We wrote the good book: instructions
for building new worlds.
Lead us not into white neighborhoods.
Deliver us from microaggressions.
Blessed are we who mourn, we who
are a blood built on a hill of embers.
We no mail-order hipster black wife.
We just trying to text our moms.
We are what we eat, leafy and anointed.
We are who we serve: banquets and bouquets
forever, foreverever, foreverever.

You may not control all the events that happen to you, but you can decide not to be reduced by them.

—MAYA ANGELOU

Natalie Rose Richardson

What do I tell the white boy who asks me of my heritage

What do I tell his mother & father
in their silver frames atop the baby grand
inside; what do I tell the tooth bleach on his sister's
sink. What do I tell his New England nose.
What do I tell the piece of uncooked pork he places
on the hot grill. What do I tell the flames that lunge
from their black mothers; what do I tell the black
mothers. What do I tell the probably-100-year
willow in his yard. What do I tell his starched polo
buttoned to Adam's apple; what do I tell the Swisher
Sweet rolled & licked in his front right pocket.
What do I tell the swamps, the long-stemmed
rice he plates in heaps; what do I tell each harvested
piece, & the water that made them & him & me
and all of us. What do I tell the blood. What do I
tell the cells of it, of him. What do I tell the ghosts
that gather & swarm to their seats at this comic scene,
white-boy-asks-brown-girl-of-heritage-in-his-million
-dollar-yard, white-boy-feigns-interest-so-as-to-get-it-in,
these ghosts in soul-slapping stitches beneath the willow;
what do I tell myself as I slip to nothing in his dark bed
-room, this stage for a cliché. What do I tell my great
-great-great whomever who stripped as I strip, who lied as I lie:
I'm so mixed up I don't even know what I am—
cue the symbol crash, cue his laughter, cue the dimming
of these terrible lights—what do I tell her, & my grandmother,
& my father, & the ones who came before me,
who came before him? What do I tell the ghosts, who
hold their applause?

Piece

From the apartment's balcony
my girlfriends and I could see
their pale skins, hear the clipped
accents. The soldiers were British
and drunk. With money flowing
the Kenyan women became
willing, every stare, every gesture
intoxicating. They tore shirts, teased
skirts, revealed panties, gyrating,
taunting those English boys who'd
never seen such chocolate breasts,
with nipples painted ebony and
hips rounded to such a swelling
you needed two hands for the grabbing
but oh, they'd heard how wild
black cats can be—scratching backs,
lusty animals in vaguely human skins.
Watching the soldiers took me back
to Ohio University's Frat Row. Those
flushed-faced men, with their backwards
baseball caps, alcohol-emboldened, leering;
the slur in their voices calling me out.
Even then, I was afraid of being that exotic,
kin to these Kenyan women. When are we not
dancing brown bodies, somewhere, swaying
for dollars or pounds, moving at whatever price
black women are selling for these days?

Nikki Wallschlaeger

Sonnet (47)

George Washington's mouth comin at you
yappin some bullshit about honesty or was
that Abe Lincoln I dunno they start to fade
into the same knockoff appropriated war
bonnet or kente cloth bathing suit worn on
Cinco de Mayo in Daytona on college break.
He kept his mouth closed because he didn't
want anyone to see us on them dollar bills
and as the rightful owner of the left tooth
I made sure to cause him a lot of trouble
on the branches of impossible roots I grew
a family of bacteria that loved to dance in
the middle of the night, especially before
a big meeting at the capitol where all the

men would gather dressed in white. We
would pound on their pots. Roast our meat.
He didn't know what to do. He'd call for his
favorite quack doctor to tend to his broken
ass—we prayed he wouldn't harm one of our
kin on the outside—but shit when a man steals
your teeth we doomed to live here. Might as
well make ourselves at home having children
keep the community going among the drool
and rot and toxic sprayed tongues we sleep
on you when we're tired, planning our escape
pulling out one plank of skin at a time, painting
with your bleeding sore gums what is going to
become common knowledge   eyeteeth

No

Your daughter cut her tongue off,
nailed it to the wall, still dripping.
Couldn't eat a thing, even sugar, even love.

She took a hungry lover
who swallowed the little light bulb
dangling from her bedroom ceiling.
The lover asked to stay.
The room kept bright.

Your daughter was spit out
& gulped up like Yordanos.
Her lover's stomach glowed
& warmed the dim rims
beneath her eyes.

When she was left alone the room got cold.
She was called selfish for not begging her lover
to stay. Her tongue, pinned into the wall,
flooded the room with blood. She had to wade.

Without the weight of her tongue
she kept nodding to everything;
she couldn't taste what she was being fed.
Love kept slipping through a hole in her throat.
She knew she had to sew her tongue back on,
before God fell out the circle in her neck.

She stumbled thru the room,
unpinned the muscle from the wall,
pulled the bright thread tight.
She kept stitching, even when

she felt her tongue was crooked.
Once her tongue was back, it slipped.
She bit it   in half.
Now, it can only hold one word.

alleged (erasure).

after Tony Medina on the Alleged Spring Break Rape, April 13, 2015
NYDAILYNEWS.COM

This,   to be   women
in   a culture of hate   hard
enough
people   stood   just feet away
 and   taped it
with their cellphones

Destiny Hemphill

shadowboxin, session one

aka shadow work

aka every tongue got to confess

aka talkin to my demons

aka talkin to myself

aka i know this ain't pretty but survival never promises to be

aka yesterday morning/ i was singin bout how i got ova/ when my voice/ cracked in the middle of my song/ & my body convulsed/ & i remembered how we ain't even got through/ today, i promised to tell the truth/ my grandmama say when i do/ the devil will be shamed/ when i do/ the demons will flee/ from me/ but my tongue got stuck/ my mouth got locked/ cuz if i'm being honest/ sometimes/ i just want em to stay/ if only just to ask em/ how they got here in the first place/ *who invited you?/ which pore did you crawl through?/* if only because, i do get lonesome sometimes/ which is to say, a lot of my folx be forgettin bout me/ it's dangerous to remember explodin stars/ aka little sad blck girls/ like me/ & i mean, at least the demons keep me company/ besides, if they leave, where shall they go? cuz since we tellin the truth & all// i am a jealous god// so if they go/ i might just follow/ please believe me/ when i say/ i haven't always been this way/ i won't always be/ but today i am/ i'll say it again/ i'll confess// i am a jealous god// i let the bile/ sit under my tongue/ i wait/ for the precise moment to/ spew it out/ please believe that/ when you hear/ the thunder clap/ it's the trauma rupturin/ my tooth crackin/ me roarin/ i'll confess/ i know i shouldn't try to possess/ nobody/ but myself/ i know nobody/ should try to possess me/ but me/ i know that what folx/ say about these demons/ possessin me/ ain't really true then/ but tell me/ what else is it that folx say?/ it's real & all—/ but it ain't true?// it's still real though// & sometimes/ i just forget/ which is more important/ to be real/ or/ to be true/& sometimes/ i just get curious/ about how you've been/ & sometimes/ i just be tired/ so i leave the door cracked open/ a lil bit/ just a lil bit/ for you/ or them/ to come through/ & honestly/ mostly/ i've been tryna quit them for a minute/ but you—you don't be callin or carin like you say you would/ & the neighbors/ they don't be callin/ or carin/ either/ & at least they/—the demons, i mean—/ still here with me// listen// sometimes/ i just wanna run away/ ain't like/ you would notice i'm missin/ cuz it ain't like/ you would be missin me/ ain't like/ you'd come lookin for me/ i mean, they the ones always lookin for me/ they the ones/ always followin/ the ones always followin/ always followin/ they the ones. always/ be followin me

Simone Savannah

beautiful black queen

Today, on my walk to the gas station for a swisher and a bottle of water, a group of men call at me from across the street. I look at them and shake my head, and when I come out of the store, I know one of them will drive their big blue truck across the street to find and follow me, and yes they pull up on me: the man with the gold horse teeth stops cuts me off with the big blue truck and they say *it's okay, it's okay, we not gone hurt you, do nuthin'* and their words echo, and a man in a neon green short sleeve shirt and matching shoes and a blue hat and square sunglasses and big round eyes gets out of the big blue truck and tells the driver with the horse teeth he can park, and he asks me my name and I tell him my name, my real name because I don't want to appear afraid, and he says something about him working up at the school and he asks me if he can see me sometimes and I want to tell this nigga to get the fuck up out my face but I tell him I have a man so he gets the message, but he still asks for my number and I tell him I'll take his instead and he asks the other man with the short hair waves and sweaty wrinkled brow to throw him his phone (he does not move his body, he keeps peering over his sunglasses with his big round eyes at me) and then he tells me something that begins with 601 and I save it as Del because he says that's his name and he asks me for a hug and I tell him *no*, and he says *that's okay I'll take one, I'll take uh hug* and I cringe when he stoops down and wraps his arms and bitter cologne around my body, and I see the two men in the truck watching and I want to know what they wonder about men and power or black men and power, about why their man wanted to touch me so badly—

after he uncloaks his body from my breasts and shoulders, he walks away and says *sawry bu' we saw uh beautiful black queen and I jus had tuh say hi, you'uh beautiful black woman,* and the men in the truck smile with their chins hanging and ask me if I have *any cuhzins.*

Divination

1.

A golden stream of fortune teller/ sits between my legs/ rubbing my
clitoris/ my magic ball of wonder/ she has in her eyes generations/
a star speckled sky/ she counts the months my husband and I have
made lightning/ hoped for rain/ danced the sheet tango/ pulled the
thorns from our lips when the blood swelled again/ this is becoming a
tradition/ this squatting and hoping the bones fall into two pink lines/
this wishbone of legs bending to break/ this awkward wrist twist/ these
soiled hands/ blossoming to nothing so often/ this time/ be more/ this
time/ be a promise waiting to bow/ be worth the 3 minute weight/ be a
nebula parting to burst/ be another set of hands/ of feet/ another mouth
to say/ Momma/ Pant/ Blink/ Breath/   Smile.

2.

I am trying not to see
your hands
in every clot

To smell your breath
the aroma
of hot blood
against cold porcelain

To look down
into this plagued river
of dreams.
Watch you drown
in the current I made

Wipe away your eyes
like they never
held my stare
or saw how beautiful I was
inside

I am trying not to
think the worst
believe you gone
cry myself under
so deep I can't breathe enough
to call
your name

3.

Since this womb has become a land
of kenopsia and ghosts
of muscles still flitter
your name

I find it hard to say
I don't remember how it feels
to have you
inside of me

This abandoned shell
has known bustle
has loved long into trimester

I have known how
to push
until it splits
me in two

But this time around
the pain is not

There was more
blood than baby

More thudding rubatosis
than movement

When the crimson
tide subsided
When the cervix
expunged your record
Contracted its lips
into a confidential file

There are memories
that still haunt me

There are handprints
plastered in a place
I can only measure
with the grief
of many moons
and irregular cycles

And no one
will call me
Mother
for this

Noname

Bye Bye Baby

Interview, interlude in the nude with my boo thang
Got the flu with the tea remedy for my boo thang
My baby needs some milk and honey
My baby needs some milk and honey
I swear he love me
My tummy almost got ready
For biddi-baby spaghetti
And teddy bear in my window now
Golden child, always smile
Before you leave, don't look down
God will help you spread your wings

My baby needs some milk and honey
My baby needs some milk and honey

Never ask me why she said goodbye
Why baby die near white walls
Cigarettes over skyfall
Writing this like this my song
Never ask me why she hesitated
Almost waited, waiting room
Playdate up to heaven soon
Soon I will see the King
He reminds me
Some get presents before they even ready
I could see that she loves me
I know her heart is heavy

Telefone-ication nation
Baby help me testify
Oooh you know I hate goodbye

Bye bye blue
Somebody let the yellow in
Bye bye blue
I'm gonna fall in love again
On a lonely road where happiness needs us
You my baby, you my baby
I'm your baby, I'm your baby
You my baby, you my baby
I'm your baby, I'm your baby
On a lonely road where happiness needs us
I'm gonna fall in love again
On a lonely road where happiness needs us

Venessa Marco

offwhite

they say I'm offwhite
high yellow, bright, bright

I do all the passing

they say my body a light
say real black and brown be shadows
cast aside
grounded
an offering to the wildest dark
and I, struttin' 'round God given
like I'm God given
like God done gave me all this sky

they say
us light skin women be church
real black and brown bodies
be four little girls
Birmingham black

when you're culturally ambiguous
the world thinks you as middle ground
as unscathed
as no one's daughter

you pretty for black
you not black enough
you better race
you exotic
wifey material

every white girl will fold to you
claim your skin a rude stain
remind you
that no matter how light you think you are
you can't sit at their table
you ain't eating their food
ain't no brown skin belly getting swollen off of no white folk

every brown girl will fold to you
claim your skin baptized and holy ridden
remind you
that no matter how brown you think you are

you can't sit at their table
you ain't eating their food
ain't no light skin belly getting swollen
it's been getting swollen by them white folks, remember?

you a footnote
a bastard child
you massa done grown weary and fucked the field negro now
you a house negro
all uppity and stainless
shucking and jiving
clean
that's what you are
golden, baby

ain't no black boy
lynched, gutted, peeled alive
spewing from your breath

ain't no black girl
raped, fucked alive
spewing from your breath

when they look at you

they cannot see blood
you are what made it
a bridge of sorts
the marriage between murderer and quest
it makes you a casualty
you're at war with yourself
when they look at you
they cannot see blood

I think of my great-great-grandmother
of her tired hands
the way my hair is silly as hers

what of your grandmother?
of the hemp knot 'round her nape
of her mutilated body
when they look at you
they cannot see blood

what a privilege!
to be a child of diaspora
marginalized like the rest of them
but too light to be thought to be marginalized like the rest of them
go 'head, baby!
play that light skin violin
cry them light skin privileged tears
death ain't coming for you

death ain't coming for you

The Holy Theatre

after Kiki Petrosino

Everything is a horcrux if you sing hard enough. I whisper
the empty, I could've rescued myself. Not just from Carrie cuts but
vibrato too if I had opened the office door sooner. I can be
honest here. I owe apologies but no one checks
the post office when you're famous. I'm terrified all the time
because it's in the director's notes. I slow dance with broken
streetlights and our haunting
sounds like I'm stepping on your toes. I can be
honest now. I sing the truth in my sleep. All the you are for lovings
get caught in my teeth. There's blood on my pillow
and stained in the sheets. Yesterday I let the truth bubble up and
slit my throat. Today, my claws unhinge my trap,
razors flood out. Here, heal means hurt, here, one thing believes
it's another. Like love and damnation or
your belt voice and better. I can say this
now. I smear my blood
in the audience's eyes and
demand. I hum the tune and Babs sings it back
over my choking. The curtain nevers.
The applause recoils but as they say, I
must go on. Spring forgets its lines and
winter steps on as understudy. Spookchill gets the best
of me and is worse
than before. Scared blinds me so bad I
don't see red: I become it.

Ajanae Dawkins

Pulling Teeth and Answers Before Dying

No Grandma, dancing on the man's
grave won't stir his ghost.
You can't get revenge on
the dead

> *All the women I know*
> *dance until their heels*
> *dig a charnel for their men.*

Yes, Grandma
he still dead.

> *I apologize to Christ*
> *for forgetting he is*
> *the only man who comes back*
> *to love us.*

No, Grandma, think about it
like this. Without his jaw
locked around that whiskey
bottle, cooling and burning
his gums while his teeth
unrooted themselves,
probably wouldn't be you
 and your six girls in Detroit.
A house you bought
with yo dime.

> *Because of her, I sovereign*

myself. Cobblestone tongue
build the road I walk on.

Probably still be Cincinnati. Still
be one bedrooms and
Girls who flinch at the front door

> *Flinching is a generational curse*
> *I don't blame her for.*

still a husband
who slurs his pockets
empty at a card table.
Debonaire and drunk on draining
himself.

> *I loved a man like this once and left before*
> *a promise of forever I could not keep.*

He so full of nothing he let
you have a clean
break. A step into a summer
night and none of him to take
with you

> *Every man I've loved left a state-sized*
> *scab I am grateful to just pick. The way*
> *my Grandma talks, her whole body was*
> *the scar.*

Grandma, you don't think that a gift?
A missing body every night? When there, an unpliable
bane on the mattress.
To make slipping away easier than the knot
on the noose

Idrissa Simmonds

Dawn Prayer Call

on the line with my dying mother
i choose words that land soft
as fingers in the sweet of her scalp.
sometime ago i became her patron saint
of hope and faith a calm weft of voice
she ascends.
her voice thick with East New York
then mine then hers again
we call and respond
our voices moving like smoke
between open mouths.

i was not holy before
i have never been a light to anyone
especially not my mother—pretty brown woman
whose body contained mine, gave me my sheen,
my breath of champale and bacon fat,
my taste for malt and sugared donuts,
my love of a well-painted face and clean brows.

i have been the worm inching through soil
not the butterfly
we are women bad things happen to.
we knot our headscarves and angle our knees
around thoughts of miracles
that will not happen.
the things we desire burn us,
crown our heads with scorn.

What i want is time to resurrect
all the days i have buried

to crawl back from the old woman
already keeping company   inside me.

we pray over the line my eyes
are wide open
i lay across an unmade bed
dawn light through the window
segmenting my flesh.

this is our audacity—
to pray for a stunning exit,
for the brittle body to rearrange itself
like a floor-length skirt
to dance
        and dance
            before death

Whitney Greenaway

Carnival Fire of '63

What I knew about the fire:

It happened on February 25th, 1963. Three men burned alive, including my grandfather's best friend Eric. My grandfather survived. My grandmother survived.

I have just asked my grandparents about the fire. It is fifty-four years later, and I worry about all the stories I haven't yet plucked from their fading memories. I know this is my own doing—somehow, believing in their immortality makes my living a little less complicated. I call home on a Sunday and they want to know why I'm asking about flames. I do not say that now it is how I stay alive. I need the heat, even if only in theory; the charred parts of myself are the ones I love best. I wonder then if it is selfish of me to hunger for this story merely for my survival, but I don't wonder too long because daddy starts talking.

What I know now:
Two days before the fire
(according to daddy):

Daddy and his *padnas*[1] gather at Eric's house on Saturday night and all of their troubles are dissolved in jokes & booze & dominoes. There are two days left until Carnival but the excitement is humming on their flesh, their eyes wide and giddy with dance. At some point, Eric asks if they want to see his *sensay*[2] outfit and they all respond affirmatively. When they descend the stairs, the costume is hard to miss: it is carefully hung over a closet door on a wooden hanger, bright white with an eerily glossy essence. Imagine a billion strips of frayed rope sewn and layered over a shirt and pair of trousers, so that they disappear and the ensemble resembles that of a large shaggy dog. Eric is proud of his costume—after all he did slave away at it himself—and the other men gape in awe. One person asks how is it that the garb is so shiny and Eric explains that after it was all sewn together, it was dipped in gasoline and voila: the shimmer. It is important to note that the material used to make the rope is already flammable so this added step for cosmetics is treacherous, much to the dismay of the men. One in particular takes a lighter to the costume and it is ablaze *"before Jack can say Robinson."* Collectively they quickly put out the flare and there is little damage to the *sensay²* but it is clear that it is a risk. Eric is unbothered, eager to sport his lustrous style on Monday afternoon. Daddy and his friends return to their drinks, and nurse them until the cocks begin to crow and the sky is cracked open by sunrise.

Two days before the fire
(according to mammy):

Mammy is at home down the road sorting baby clothes when she comes across my grandfather's *sensay²* pieces. She is three months with child and annoyed. Her husband is not home, she is alone with this small belly and two toddlers and is struggling to stay afloat emotionally. It is a predominantly patriarchal society so she does not have the luxury of complaints; she cannot expect her husband to be home helping to mind the children—not at any time, but especially not two nights before all the action. She sighs in exasperation because here are Lovertie's crocus bag pieces scattered among her freshly washed baby clothes. Daddy's *sensay²* differs from that of Eric's in two ways: first, the material used is unweaved bags predominantly used for storing and transporting rice and sugar—a milder substitute for the rope that Eric has used. Secondly, daddy has opted to wear only a jacket of the covered material, as opposed to a full body suit. All of this to say: his costume would not be as heavy as Eric's, which is ironic in itself because mammy tells me that the reason Eric wanted to try the rope *sensay²* this year is that the crocus bag outfit proved too too hot and heavy in prior years. So here she is picking crocus bag pieces from layette and cloth diapers. She retires early to bed, soon after the toddlers and she is wishing for morning, and night, and morning and night, and morning and night and morning again so Carnival will be over and her husband will be home, even if only to bury himself in the belly of cars and vodka.

The day of the fire
(according to daddy):

A little before midmorning, not long after the last of the *j'ouvert*[3] revelers have stumbled home, sweaty and drunk on alcohol or music, or both, my grandfather walks up the road to Eric's mother-in-law's house only to determine what time the gang would head to town in costume. The veranda is empty and only silence greets his raps on the wooden front door, so he makes his way back home but runs into Eric who tells him he has just come from church. My grandfather questions this peculiar act but Eric is nonchalant about the novena he just finished and insists it is no big deal. Daddy says in retrospect it was as if Eric knew he needed to make peace with God before he died.

Not long after this encounter, the crowd of approximately six men, all donned in some version of *sensay*[2], dance their way through the streets of *Roseau*[4], the *lapokabwit*[5] drumming in their blood and they drink from flasks filled with everything but juice and water. It is Carnival Monday on the island and the sidewalks are filled with spectators admiring the parade, chipping along to the music, and glistening in the sun. Daddy and his friends stop for about half an hour to eat, having their fill of someone's roadside *pelau*[6] and everyone has the kind of laughter with no end. They head back out to the King George V street close to two o'clock and are moving with the beat when it happens. My grandfather hears "VOOP" and in the second it takes him to turn around he sees three of his friends, including Eric practically engulfed in flames. He rushes in and in an effort to help, his jacket catches fire and all of a sudden there are other men holding him down. They are taking off his flaming jacket, the music has stopped and only screams pierce the afternoon sky. He doesn't remember much else after that, only seeing Martin charred on the roadside. He makes his way to nurse's house where he meets my worried grandmother and together they learn that the other two men have been taken to the hospital.

The day of the fire
(according to mammy):

The day was typical in the house even for a holiday like Carnival Monday. The babysitter was helping with the children, and my grandmother was just finishing lunch preparation in the kitchen. She showered and decided she would go to *Roseau*[4] alone to watch part of the parade. She had only just gotten to town when someone screamed: *"mi yo ka bwilay moun ah bah la! Gwo difay!* (translation: Look! They're burning people down there! Big fire!). Mammy starts walking a little faster in the pointed direction and the closer she gets, the more screams she hears. At this point she has heard that the men on fire are those in *sensay*[2] and her heart is now pounding. She is trembling with dread, making her way through onlookers, one hand fiercely protecting her small rounded belly, the other tensed on her side. She passes Martin near the gutter and she notices he is burnt to a crisp. She compared his carcass with that of a roasted pig: the way the mouth shrinks and the teeth are dazzling white. She hurries along, searching frantically for daddy and I am unable to imagine that panic. Finally someone ushers her to nurse's house and assures her that her husband is alive, unharmed. She does not believe it until she sees him sauntering towards the porch, half-naked and somber. She does not hear the howling or the sirens. She only hears herself: *merci Bondye, merci Bondye, merci Bondye* (translation: thank you Jesus, thank you Jesus, thank you Jesus).

The aftermath
(according to mammy and daddy):
There have been three funerals all within a week of each other. The two men who did not immediately succumb to their injuries were eventually flown to Jamaica for more advanced medical care. Eric's wife called home one day to say Eric was improving and was looking his best on the day he passed. My grandfather has never been the man to dwell in sorrow but he goes to all three burials and vows to never *play mas* again.

I talk of my grandmother's survival even if she wasn't a victim of the fire. Not everyone is able to survive trauma; those who claw their way out often have trouble living. The boy child she carried was born in August and is sometimes frightened in his sleep. She's convinced that his small body remembers the fear that coursed through her that dreadful afternoon. She holds his name in her mouth like a prayer, and traces crosses on his chest as if to ward off spirits.

If you are familiar with Caribbean people and their gossip, you know the millions of theories presented about what really happened that day. Who knew the flammability of the costumes? Was the fire intentional?

Was it an accident? Did the costume make contact with a cigarette butt? Fifty-four years later and those questions are still looming; even after an out-of-town detective named Slater was hired to conduct an investigation, there was never enough evidence to quell the rumors. Don't a lot of things end that way? In uncertainty? And doesn't life go on?

————

padnas¹: a friend, usually male.

sensay²: a costume of West African descent, usually worn during Carnival. The attire can be made from strips of cloth, paper, banana leaves, rope, or frayed plastic sacks.

j'ouvert³: literally meaning opening of the day, this refers to the official start of Carnival, the last Monday before the Lenten season.

Roseau⁴: the capital of Dominica.

lapokabwit⁵: literal translation is goat's skin, but the term refers to music created as a collective result of drums and homemade instruments.

pelau⁶: a West Indian one pot dish consisting of brown stewed chicken, rice, and lentils or pigeon peas.

I am not wrong:

Wrong is not my name

My name is my own

my own

my own

—JUNE JORDAN

Jamila Woods

N

at christmas my mother giggled like a girl
when she told us her father's nickname
for chestnuts   *Nigga toes.* my mother
never musters more than the first letter
of a cuss. her mother used soap to clean
out mouths. her father was in the navy
texas, new hampshire, okinawa
my mother always the only *N* in class.

at church i studied diction. Black people
never say *good* when you ask how we're doing
we say *fine.* never ask grandma if she's mad
dogs are mad, i'm angry she'll say. say *watchacalma*
when you don't know someone's name. say *oh my stars*
instead of the lord's name in vain.

everybody in church was black, but the stained glass
had a white jesus. it begged the question, *what would jesus do*
when singing along to a rap song, could he stop himself?

i've been called *nigger* once in my life.
a car full of white boys at a stop sign
outside my house. i was eight. the only
bad word I knew was *ass.* i'd learned it
from a mary chapin carpenter song. they pulled up
& spat *hey nigger.* i shouted *ass . . . holes!*
it felt like using a butter knife to cut tough meat.

at a rap show in milwaukee a sea of white
heads bobbed as i watched their lips trace the word
eager and easy as if it meant hello in a new country

white people are lazy thieves, they mispronounce
Black names but love a reason to sing *Nigga* loudly

listening to a tribe called quest in the corner
i try to earn my grandfather's tongue. *Nigga*
is a tonal language. i don't say *Nigga*
in public cause i'm a perfectionist, same way
i wouldn't hold a snake if i didn't know exactly how.

whoever i am, i am always Black, practicing
our surname under my breath like a poem
i already wrote but have yet to read out loud.

Justice Ameer

(After God Herself)

Adam ate an apple
it got stuck in his throat
and they called him Eve
the progenitor
the creator of all things
the mother of strength
and fortitude
and sadness
Adam ate an apple
choked on it so hard
a rib popped out of his chest
and they called it Eve
the progenitor
the creator of all things
the mother of strength and fortitude
and sadness
it takes the hacking of a body
to make a woman
Adam hacking up a piece of his body
it was just a piece of fruit
they called me fruit once too
they called me fruity
before they called me flaming
before they called me faggot
before they called me woman
i thought i would have
to hack this body into pieces
woman, a name stuck in my throat
right under the apple Adam tried to eat
choked on it for years
waited for my ribs to pop out

my chest to explode
for my Eve to be created
from the fruit i couldn't swallow
they called me fruit once
until they called me woman
and then they just called me fruitless
as if it took a womb to be
progenitor
creator
mother of all things
strength and fortitude and sadness
they reckon God looked
at the image of herself
and called it Adam
they still don't call me woman
they still don't birth me Eve
even though they cast me out
my throat shrunken close
with the fruit still stuck in it
like Adam
before they called him Eve
and suddenly i am a stranger
to Eden
i am a stranger to this body
as if it hadn't always been mine
i reckon God looked
at the image of herself
and called it me
but i don't know if that
was before or after the apple
before or after Adam choked
which came first
the progenitor or the mother
the apple or the rib
the strength or the sadness
this body was God's original creation
but they called it sin
they called it Adam

I reckon God looked
at the image of herself
and called Adam Eve
after she choked on his name
some fruit that bloomed
in everyone else's throat
but she could never quite swallow
the fall of man was an apple
hacked up from a fruitless body
a woman learning what evil was
like a man forcing his name upon you
the fall of man was a rib
being torn from a chest
and men calling that violence holy
naming a woman based only
on the body parts she's made of
the fall of man
was the beginning of Eve
Eve casting out Adam's name
Eve discovering who she was
the progenitor
the creator of all things
the mother of strength
and fortitude
and sadness
the fall of man
was Eve becoming a woman
with or without Eden's approval
and now
every time someone
tries to call her Adam
tries to force the apple
of his name down her throat
she laughs
she swallows
she looks at God herself
and she smiles

Cuero

Language: Spanish

Etymology: From Latin *Corium* ("skin. the hide that covers a beast. leather. stark naked.")

Pronunciation: "Cuero": \ kwe.ro\

Noun:

1. a regular girl. a girl in pocket-less jeans. a girl with long hair. a girl with a nose ring. a girl with a lip ring. a girl with a tongue ring. a girl with earrings, any ring but a diamond on her left hand. a girl in skirts. Shorts. Tank tops. Spaghetti straps. 2. a spectacular girl; with hips that look like water waiting to be spilled into the cupped hands of the thirsty. a cuero lets the world know she is hot. She can feel the sun. a cuero nail files her sweet tooth. 3. a cuero might be a plain girl; nothing llamativo—a forgotten girl. Forsaken. Who parts her hair down the middle. Who doesn't have cleavage. Whose mouth doesn't look like it is forever waiting.

As in "Look at that cuero. Ain't she loose? Tied down by nothing. Waving in the wind."

Safia Elhillo

self-portrait
with the question of race

عِرق: /'i·riq/ *n.* race; vein; *SUDANESE COLLOQUIAL derogatory* african blood; black blood.
الله يسود ليلتك زي ما سود وجهك "may god darken your nights/ as he has darkened your face"

اسمرت: /as·ma·rat/ *v. FEMALE THIRD PERSON SINGULAR PAST TENSE* to tan; to get darker.
egyptian comedian mohamed henedi dresses as a sudanese man & sings "وسمرت وإتحرقت بس بطاطا" "she got darker/ & burned like a potato"

[but your daughter will be fine but keep her out of the sun but do something with that hair   or people will not know she is بنت عرب *daughter of arabs*]

La Negra Takes Medusa
to the Hair Salon

and the salonist from Santiago runs her fingers through the serpents. *It'll be extra for la monstra,* she tells La Negra, *her snakes, they hiss and squirm too much.* It takes the salonist hours to bend the snakes around the rollers, make them still beneath the hairnet.

And later. The dryer bell dings. The snakes have grown sleepy, easier for the salonist to drag the brush through Medusa's scalp with one hand, lulling the snakes straight with the blower in the other. The last of them uncoil and hang limply down Medusa's back.

Oh, don't she look so much better! The women in rollers croon, *Una propia tigerasa.* They comment on how the snakes' eyes have been seared and swollen shut, how their tongues swing gently from their mouths, their fangs bent loose by the small-tooth comb.

And although Medusa can't possibly understand the cadence of el Cibao, she fingers her half-dead snakes, holds one up to her mouth,

ay Negra, ay Negra, she doesn't say.

Yesenia Montilla

Confession #1

If I knew back then that I'd one day be a poet
That one day my words would matter
That one day I might mean something to someone
I might not have had that abortion in '93. Or maybe
I would have, but under a different name. Anne
Sexton taught me everything about lust and shame
but nothing about regret. No matter, when they ask
why I did it, I'll tell them I was young
& I desperately wanted the fruit to fall far
from the tree, that is to say, my mother's face
is a red stone and I wanted to be a diamond—

Love On Flatbush Avenue

Because the roach had wings and tore thru our crib like a landlord or
ghost and you screamed first even though i saw it first heading for the
light and it hid behind the white curtain or it colonized the whole window
and promised to never die and because it's been nearly five years of my
mouth on your mouth and your mouth and your mouth i knew what i hafta
do so i took the bougie 7th generation cleaning solution that we buy cuz
we concerned about our carbon footprint and i spray and spray and spray
and punctuate each one with a scream and repeat about 11 times before
the roach slows its juke and i hit him with something who can say what
just something that is not my hand or my new clogs or my anything i love
or use to love and i scream how *the roach looks like shrimp* and i hear
you laughing now from the other end of the apartment you are like really
feeling yourself you chortle so much it sound like all your ancestors

done joined you and i yell from the landlord's new room *what's funny
bitch?* and boy that really does it cuz here you go peeling and peeling
giggles outchyo mouth and here go your Savta Bea guffawing right along
with you i mean carrying on your Getzel's there too i know because you
are laughing with all your teeth and whole belly and the now ruined bug is
spread across the wall and i holler and think it should be chalkoutlined
but i bag it and run snorting and laughing too and my snot is stuck in the
bridge of my nose and i run some more down the hallway and out the
front door and down the steps and now all my people are with me Delcie
and Ellie Pearl and James Ganzi and we running like we got wings and
know where the light is and i throw the dearly departed into the bins on
Flatbush and maybe it's raining a little and so my afro is soggy when i
return to you and rinse my hands in the busted bathroom sink and i look
at you and think it's such a good thing to pick your own life

    O, tonite i killed a thing cuz you are not from
    a killing people and we pant with our own

jokes and inherited tongues and we
tangle our separate homes together.

Love and Water

after Nabila Lovelace

I am just like anyone else, I need love and water.
                                   —**Prince**

Never stay with the man who fucks you
and does not keep water in his refrigerator.
Cotton mouth latched to the tap in a silver kitchen.
How original. You are thirsty and your pussy
is wet. Even that is a failing. You suck the valve until
every pipe in the city is dry, and somehow you are
the one left rusting from the inside, out. Like everyone else,
you need love and water to survive. And which can he give to you?
His cum is so damp and stagnant, silverfish grow between your tired legs.
A nerve in your tooth browning the moment he pulls out. Your pussy
is so good, and you know it. But even good can be improved.
Perhaps you did not give your best. Maybe you didn't fry the chicken hard
enough. He chewed the tacky, pink meat and was unimpressed.
It is possible that when you called him daddy he remembered the abortion
and was disgusted by you, all over again.
Still you begged him to stay, until you sweated out
your perm. All that lye in his sheets making the bedroom
smell like a human scalp was burning. It was.

Simone Savannah

Look:

splits so deep
my pussy kisses
the blue yoga mat / i came up in here with
bitch   you so average:
cat cows / backbends / sun salutations: gained

I : born this way : double-dutched double-jointed blood / black girl /
    Gabby girl / black magic
thick thighs yes stretch too   hips mimic elastic / I : breathe and
    slip / sustain
the weight of your instructions in my wrists—
in child's pose   I   worship Misty's
tip   toe   ball-pointed calves
ask her to   forgive me   for
being
here
and no longer
dancing

before
you want me : eyes locked on my contortion
say *how beautifully limber*
then, you: yoga-trained / body forced / skin thinned
flip through *Yoga Journal* / study my *hypermobility*:
practice my body in your bedroom mirror / tell me
watch your knees / try not to hyperextend / rise
to correct me / say I must
get headaches from good sex and stretching / say
also *be sure to level your hips* / as if
it is my first time / blooming into half moons
you couldn't imagine

you think
god must have birthed broken brown bodies
forgot to thread the joints of all the blue black trap niggas—

Look here : I'm a don't-need-a-strap-nigga
core strength so live
padangustasana so steady / twisted
in eagle pose / my eyes closed / you watch me
          exhaled a standing split / when i used to strip / tipped
twenties stuck to the back of my thighs / still
not afraid of my body :
yoga right next to you
like I'm your 500-hour teacher
last name like your Savasana
yoga right next to you
cuz
I'm even savage in mudras

and yo ya man in the back
twists his neck to see me without permission
after class tells me he can't help but watch me in the mirror
wants to know what else stretches that wide—
sweetheart how long you been into this
cause you do it so easy
wonders if I saw Serena's match that day
you must be her sister Venus
he says
body
a hot
yoga train of flesh
he reaches out to touch me

destiny, chile

i am just a regular ho i just suck [at] regular things i just wear scraps of
style i smell like bath and body works new nag champa appropriated
musk soap baby pink

i like my cereal soggy and my liquor irate
i like sweat-stain stories and each daybreak punctured with slamming
doors that shake up buildings
mi nuh cyar if yuh neighbor angry

i'm a regular ho
i have names they are majestic they be ancestral they too hard to
pronounce this is only
my
third baptism

i got a library full of bibles and clinic receipts and Fanon and
hee hee hee i can match u tit for tat i'm so regular

there are things I like I couldn't tell u. they are secrets of deepest
underworld they make spike lee confused with purpose they are things
that burn yo scalp and fetishize your eyes make u wonder
bout yo decision to wrap me up in soundbooth and
barbed wire

i got secrets that hide under the rusted row aisle at the beauty supply
next to rat tail/ get on yo knees and look then

i know some things that might just flip yo shit/ I know trump is a
whimperer/ i know what make u get off

U cant just ask me u cant speak to me directly u not citizen of my state u

not witness
u not protected
who this ho they ask
i answer regular, with litanies of apostrophes   guide you along

but they just mad there are things I don't tell, my naked only stop at
skin, i know some things

i cant tell u
my granny might be reading

                    And snitches get stitches

Brittany Rogers

My daughter prays
for a brother, and gets one

And the whole world, it seems
says congratulations.
Says I got lucky   this time
that girl must have a direct line to God
look how He blessed me
to not birth something black and female
and poison tongued   again.

Them boys, they say, ain't no trouble.
No worrying about breasts or wanting or
bleeding or babies.

Them boys they say, love
you even when they turn
beer gut and testosterone.

Them girls, on the other hand be
rattlesnakes in a foreign habitat.
Uncontained gasoline. Spreading.
Matches in they fingertips—no
ambulance in sight.

I'm sure you didn't want another daughter
anyway. Them black girls got
tongues like cars swerving
in traffic. Hair a cacophony
of coil and downed wire.
Who tryna wade through all those tangles
and emotion? All they feelings

dirty words. And those girls,
they sneaky, a footstep you never hear
coming. The alley cat that doesn't get
invited in for dinner.

They say boys so much easier.
That I would have spent all my toil on
her, had she been. They forget they talkin
to a woman made of black
sea and failed curses. Forget I
was somebody's plea for a
son returned void.

I was **a new person** then, I knew things I had not known before, I knew things that you can know only if you have been through what I had just been through.

—JAMAICA KINCAID

Aracelis Girmay

sister was the wolf

sister was the wolf
& could cross easily through

the mountain dark to den
keen & quivered with

the muscular siege of slit   purse
purple with hours

purse purple with birthwork
her sight both inward-

& outward-lit
on what small sparkle of pyrite

in the silt or the thick smell of her own
wilderness opening shit & hair & blood

each little birth
an astonishment of form

inside its own tiny veil
licked toward the air of this Other Side

    [*Live!*]

then that sound
from the hospital's infant table

after what seemed like years
of silence   a mew

which held inside it
all the voices of

this dream & other animals
trying to begin

Elizabeth Acevedo

Mami Came to this Country as a Nanny

and around the same time she tells me i can't walk
the house wearing only panties anymore,
she teaches me how to hand wash them in the sink.
tsking that washing machines
don't launder as well as a good knuckling,
she drops soap on the crotch, folds the fabric
on itself and shows me how one end
pulls out the stains of the other;
detergent, and fabric, and hands against hands
make the seemingly most dirty material clean again.
no menstrual cycle ever made me more woman
in mami's eyes than this learning how to wash my own ass,
this turning of the shower rod into a garland of intimates—
this memory tightens my fist that first week of freshman year
when caitlyn kerr's mother, who has a throat made for real pearls,
points her unsoftened mouth at me, letting loose the sullied words:
you better take care of caitlyn, she's always had help.
and i have to blink, and blink, and blink but leave unmentioned
all the ways my hands have learned to care for things like her.

Birth, mark

when i think i am not my mother's child,
my mouth betrays me, i carry her
fuck you flung at my face
a knuckle in my cheekbone, i spit out fingers.
she gave me a crescent scar, swung a wire hanger
across, *i should have had the abortion*
your low-life father wanted,
drags me by my rag-doll heart each time,
passes a palm down her stomach,
lifts her shirt above the waist,
yells *look at me, look at the damage—*
i came into this world a stain, a stone, a c-section
the soft terror fleshed out of her body.
i could have stayed in there forever,
stretched her skin into translucence, my window
seat to pastoral weeping, i left her
underbelly glistening
the welt of a wound worn,
withdrawn, shrinking into—
i watched her smear cocoa butter
above her hips, hands pulsing of vines
along the groove of striae, tending the umber
lightning bolts in the rhythm of pouring,
of my being here.
i am the sort of animal that needs to be held,
ruins the hold, tears the body apart
limb by limb, satin strands of skin ripped open
suffer, shame, sacrifice hum in the head
as if heirloom or honor or hurt—
a vexed tongue can be a pistol, a loaded barrel of insults
can be ears bleeding. a testimony of regret

unborns *you*
ungrateful piece of
when they were two bodies laid together
heaving each other's breath
did my parents pause to make me?
i want to hunt down the second
just before
and live in the *i love you,* of the quiver.
was it rapture or mere spasm?
did they pray, did they exhale
did they say *amen?*

Blue Magic

As she parted my hair into four, I was a poem
in need of revision, too small for wigs like

she and the sweet-scented churchwomen wore
so I sat on the vinyl kitchen floor, my arms holding

tight to knees as she yanked away
nappy coils and pressed them into ponytails

of dark ribbon. On Saturday afternoons, the kitchen
doubled as beauty shop, the gas stove an incense burner

smoking hot combs, curling rods and hair. Gladys sat
in a black lacquered chair, paid on lay-a-way from working

in the backs of restaurants and cleaning the insides
of toilets for white folks. It was honest work

for an honest person trying to make it in the world
and have a little left over. How happy she was

that one morning to place under the Christmas tree
my very own doll, one to sit with over the weekends

and do its hair. And I wonder how she felt when I
demanded she return the nylon haired plastic doll

for a white one. I didn't want something that needed
a grandmother, that needed hot combs and hair grease.

Sometimes you can watch a person age, the face

displays the cinematic reel of history, of white sheets

burnt cross and blackface. She returned the doll
and I remember her more silent than usual. At that

moment in the car I was any girl, from
el barrio or the hood or the rez, any brownish girl riding

with her grandmother as the car inched away from the store lot
families coated and gloved rushing with bags to and fro

snow falling and eyes facing forward, while each
wiper in the windshield dragged itself along.

Chick

On Pike Street we slip and slide on blue black garbage bags
made slick by green hoses. The boys try to impress you. Their flat
stomachs collide with wet plastic, the suction welting their skin.
You are the risk for them to catapult limbs across sopping grass.
Pressing fingers into the flesh at your elbow, they hold you steady.
I watch their eyes trace rivulets down the curve of your spine, the splay
of your hips. You can make your body an alphabet. My flesh folds and flops.
Does not move in a rhythm that makes these young men cry out. Spider
fingered stretch marks palm the small of my back, veins wait to burst purple
rivers along my legs. I know the way fat girls shrink, curl the mass
of their bodies into a cocoon praying for big breasts and hips. I want
to make the boys swoon. I want them to touch me, the peach fuzz
of their upper lips coaxing my dimples from hiding. I wonder what their
mouths taste like. I would eat them only to find out they were rotten at the
center.

Safia Elhillo

self-portrait with dirty hair

trying to flatten the jagged curl i hear my great-grandmother *she's a pretty girl but why do you let her go outside like that people will think she does not have a name* i hear my grandmother trying to explain away all my knots *her mother took her to america it is different she does not know anymore how to look done* i hear my mother trying not to hurt my feelings but unable to escape how her mother raised her *habiba you always look nice but today you look maybe a little tangled* i hear a man i don't love begging me to undo my braid to show his friends *my girl got a waterfall* i watch halim sing to a creamcolored girl i hear the quiet ripple of her loose waves i get searched to the scalp at airport security i wear my hair big & loose & free of the straightening iron to my cousin's wedding & grandma says *you might as well have just shown up in pajamas*

A sestina for a black girl who does not know how to braid hair

Your hands have no more worth than tree stumps at harvest.
Don't sit on my porch while I make myself useful.
Braid secrets in scalps on summer days for my sisters.
Secure every strand of gossip with tight rubber bands of value.
What possessed you to ever grow your nails so long?
How can you have history without braids?

A black girl is happiest when rooted to the scalp are braids.
She dances with them whipping down her back like corn in winds of
    harvest.
Braiding forces our reunions to be like the shifts your mothers work, long.
I find that being surrounded by only your own is more useful.
Gives our mixed blood more value.
Solidifies your place with your race, with your sisters.

Your block is a layered cake of your sisters.
Forced your lips quiet and sweet and they'll speak when they need to
    practice braids.
Your hair length is the only part of you that holds value.
The tallest crop is worshipped at harvest.
So many little hands in your head. You are finally useful.
Your hair is yours, your hair is theirs, your hair is, for a black girl, long.

Tender-headed ass won't last 'round here long.
Cut your nails and use your fists to protect yourself against your sisters.
Somehow mold those hands useful.
Your hair won't get pulled in fights if they are in braids.
Beat out the weak parts of the crops during harvest.
When they are limp and without soul they have value.

If you won't braid or defend yourself what is your value?
Sitting on the porch until dark sweeps in needing to be invited, you'll be
    needing long.
When the crop is already used what is its worth after harvest?
You'll learn that you can't ever trust those quick to call themselves your
    sisters.
They yearn for the gold that is your braids.
You hold on your shoulders a coveted item that is useful.

Your presence will someday become useful.
There will be one day the rest of your body will stagger under the weight
    of its value.
Until then, sit in silence in the front with your scalp on fire from the braids.
I promise you won't need anyone too long.
One day you will love yourself on your own, without the validation of
    sisters.
No longer a stump wailing for affection at harvest.

Wading
(Ode to an Almost First Kiss)

He was one of the only
black boys in school,
older, an athlete
I, seventeen, un-kissed, and waiting
on the beach and now
a better time than ever
to learn what my friends had been
telling me about for years.

We watched waves spill onto the sand,
sand drink its clumsy offering,
my wanting making a mouth
out of everything,
even the moon laughed at us,
two kids whose skin mimicked its sky.

He fumbled with the moment,
heavy enough to create a tide,
and broke as he told me
he preferred the light shore
of my friend's skin instead,
I waded as my disappointment was
swallowed by ocean.

He was not the first or only
boy to leave me buoyed
the one before him was
anonymous valentine,
with no lighthouse to guide me

I spent my freshman year
guessing his name

The one after him was a
dark corner at a party
he touched me on purpose, but
walked by me in hallways
without saying a word,
I, unable to look at him
without tasting salt.

For a black girl in my town
you learned the worth of your body
by the number of boys who
wanted you, but didn't ask you out.
Your color, clandestine,
unworthy of public sparkle,
the kind that dances
on surface of The Sound

As a black girl in my town,
you dance on your own.
Shame your body for wanting
anyone to touch you, validate you,
your dignity and humanity,
colliding horizons that
create sharp reflections
of yourself

All I wanted was to look in
the mirror and be soft;
even glass thrown into the sea
takes 30 years to be beautiful,
but for me, waiting to be wanted,
no more righteous
than giving all my edges
to undeserving hands.

With this boy, I was happy
just to have hands that looked like my own
maybe then, his, more willing to hold on
though still, like always, the ocean
releases and releases

And I wonder, what moon
these boys were slaves to,
that they kept spitting me out
what shattered images of themselves
did they see as its light burned
their surface?
How bright that it blinded them
as I disappeared in my own dark?
Too black to shine
to move a body, pull it in close
I learned, black girls not worthy of the gravity
that overwhelms a heart
even when the boy, too, like tarred sky,
forgetting me makes him feel mighty,
an ocean, and I drowned
without ever touching him.

Ciara Miller

Poet Imagines Creating Full House in Rockwell Gardens

In this house, I am Danny Tanner.
My three daughters, sister, & best friend sleep
on the 2nd floor. We hug & sometimes just walk away
when we can't find the right, frustrated words to say
"I love you." This is not an actual house. I am the mother.
There are 12 floors in this building. When we can't find the right,
frustrated words to say, "I love you," we curse each other
or punch blood into thin walls. This is Rockwell Gardens.
The projects. My daughters are called white girls. They mutter "bitch"
beneath breath when I make them read *The Bluest Eye* in a building
of walls so thin, they can hear our neighbor, Jimmy, ball up
his newspaper to swat his bitch like a fly. When we can't find
the right frustrated words to say, "you've hurt me," we crack
jokes into floors so thin, even the downstairs toddlers can hear
the humbug of our laughter. The city's project is to tear Rockwell
Gardens down, to scatter us like mice, to build condominiums
over our bones. But we grew in that garden. Felt
the bite of winter & wilted from summer heat. Yet, even the leaves
crinkled & blew away, like we would, only returning in the fall
to briskly walk repaved sidewalks & it could never be a full house.
Jimmy swatting his bitch is louder than the memory
of ice cream trucks & if I could scrape together enough pennies to buy
my daughters a popsicle, I swear, would save that change, anyway,
to move us out.

Boxes of Andromeda

There are no such things as domestic goddesses
anymore. Sundays aren't filled with radio static and good

R&B. No lemon Pledge/ dust rag/ t-shirt remnants.
There are no more altars.

In my house there never were. My mother, hearty
Midwesterner, swathed in sleeveless work

shirts and steel-toed boots was not delicate.
She was not always clean.

She chained to a rock of dust and soot
and manual labor; chained to early morning

piece work; and desperate need for overtime.
My mother was a goddess of rough heels and unpainted toes.

Nothing sweet about the sweat clinging to her armpits
and forearms and breasts and back

and a forehead creased and pinched
and all things pained at the end of the day.

Each night her head lolled against the back of the sofa, snapping
back when she felt herself falling. Snapped back because the rock

of dust and soot and manual labor never quite left her skin. Was not quite
hidden by the plum lipstick puckering her mouth or the fleeting hints

of perfume that lingered longer in the bathroom then it did on her flesh.
But she was woman. She was god. Mule and spike and post and pine.

A cobble of things lifted and stored, but not delicate.
A woman commanding space in circles manual labor afforded.

That piece work allowed. That over time the overtime let her
daughter know the joys of hands free of callous and a whole body.

To know the sleep of falling.
To know the snap of falling.
To know the altar and the pearl.

Amerikkkana

On September 11th I was 7 years old holding a bowl of carrots. I had gotten a detention slip that day and the biggest worry was how hard the back of my father's hand would be when he saw it.

My father doesn't look at anyone when the telly is on. He becomes a vortex at best. A frightened Hillary Clinton type runs into the camera as smoke sinks its soft teeth into everything around her. A week ago I had read about Jeanne Claude and Christo covering skyscrapers and bridges with miles of silk. I wondered if magicians flew planes, if everyone inside had really just tumbled into a velvet sack, if giant white rabbits would line the streets of New York when the grey cleared. I thought about the concrete bungalows and permanently water-stained apartment buildings in Lagos. No plane would waste its time kissing the walls like that. The glass was much harder back home. My father turned to me unprompted. "You ok?" he asked. I put the slip behind my back.

At school they taught us a new word. "Terrorism" bends through the lips so softly you'd hardly know the meaning the first time. Mr. O said it during morning chapel and it sounded like the flu. The next week, they told us about jihad and the end of times. I packed myself nice lunches, it was an exceptionally beautiful September. I won the science fair the next month and we started doing bomb drills. I didn't try to tell my father about our daily lectures on terrorism, there were too many syllables and he really only wanted to know my maths score. What does terrorism even mean to a man who knows his colonizer's anthem better than his father's eulogy? Or a girl with two passports and an oil-rich allowance?

In the car, I vocalize along with Fela, my hips bumping on beat against the seat belt constraints, my fingers dancing on the dial to turn it up. Uncle perks up, reclines his chair forward. "Wow, Tolu, you know this?!" I smile and continue singing. "But you can't know what it means?" I falter a little, the blow strikes between my neck and ear. I explain that I do, that I speak the language and love it. He gives a small smile, the same one the tour guide gives when the whitefolk start to list their African friends and nannies, asking if he knows one of the three million Tayo's in the world. I hate feeling like a fisherman in my own blood. America swims into my lungs, I cough up border fences and visas. Dual citizenship molds my clothes, I am never on dry land.

One night, my cousins and I roam the streets of Lagos. The vendors draw soup from their pots, we argue over prices. I drool over a golden pile of jollof rice, peppered and garnished with bitter leaf. After picking up a few drinks, we wander home in a parade of gas street lamps, sweltering music, and the thick smell of maggi in everything. My cousins speak only English to me, bending their r's around a western parody accent. They give me the biggest piece of meat and bottled water. I want to scrub my entire education from my tongue, give only talking drum parties when I speak. I want to be African without two sugars and cream, I want to be black without betrayal.

Halcyon Kitchen

Granma cautioned in a kitchen off Century and Hoover,
Never throw your hair away. Burn it. 'Til yellow
cornbread bakes and greens release pot liquor,
her garnet-polished fingers unraveled each cornrow.

*Never throw your hair away, burn it 'til yellow
flames flick up and turn orange, blue.* Overhead,
her garnet-polished fingers unraveled each cornrow,
wrestling. I reminisce, standing over her deathbed.

Rain picks up and turns ochre, blue. Unsaid
were simple things. Oxtail stew and yam
recipes I recollect, standing over her deathbed.
She smoked Mores leaning in the kitchen doorjamb,

when simple things—oxtail stew and yam
recipes—were not measured nor written. Cooking while
she smoked More's leaning in the kitchen doorjamb,
her left hand in the profound curve of her hip. She'd say, *Chile,*

ma recipes are not measured nor written. Cooking while
I sat alongside the stove waiting for the hot comb, meantime
her left hand in the profound curve of her hip, she'd say, *Chile,*
I may be dead and gone, but you mark my words. Sometime

I sat alongside the stove waiting for the hot comb, meantime
I loved watching her smoking, cooking, talking with More fingers,
I may be dead and gone, but you'll mark my words. This time,
she is quiet. I hold maroon-polished hands as her soul lifts, waits, lingers.

I loved watching her smoking, cooking, talking with More fingers.
Halcyon rain picks up, soaks me blue. Nothing unsaid.
She is quiet. I hold maroon-polished hands as her soul lifts, waits, lingers,
restful. I'm remembering—standing over her deathbed.

Girdle

My grandmother packs her tetas
into a bra the size of a potato sack.
She makes us pause our game of
Super Mario Brothers to connect
its five hundred hooks.
The three of us use our bodies
to stretch the material into a forklift.
The littlest uses his three-year-old hands
to grab grandma's ass
and push it into the air.
I use my jumping on the bed
muscles to stretch fabric around
the cinnamon donuts of her back.
Grandma's bra is angry.
We are flung to the floor
laughing and screaming.
The middle one furls his brow,
declares grandma's bra is broken forever.
We stretch, pull, and push
her tumbles of woman.
Powdered fingerprints freckle her back.
We just want to play Nintendo.
Why is the universe against us?
The first hook is always hardest.
The three of us gather
at the center of her back, stitch her in.
The littlest one pats her bottom.
Finally grandma agrees with us.
He places his hand on her
new belly and reports
Grandma,
you are fat.

Naomi Extra

My Favorite Things

Seeing how many rocks can fit
up my brother's nose or what
happens if I swing a stray cat in circles.
If I shut the door of my bright
lemon drop bedroom I can
hump the sheets wonderfully
before anyone notices I'm gone.
When company is desired,
I scream at the window of
the white girl from next door until
her mother comes out. We pee in a bush
together while discussing whose urine is
yellower. Her vagina looks like rice and I
want to ask to see it again.
But I never do. If I'm feeling vindictive
I dig a hole and put my brother's favorite
playing cards in it. I look for them a week
later while dad is looking for his car keys.
I yell about poop in the grocery store.
Big poop, stinky poop, who pooped,
poopy head and how many poops.
If no one is paying attention I call 911 and hang up
(blame it on my brother).
Eat all the Freihofer's cookies (blame that on
my brother too).
Color in my *Snow White* coloring book
and hit anyone who rips out the pages.
Eat peanut butter and Fluff with
the Italian girl down the road
whose house is bigger
than my entire apartment building.

In the middle of the night I
watch Lifetime movies about women in prison
and don't cover my eyes during the sexy parts.
On the way to school I sing
"Lets Talk About Sex" and get smacked. I tell little
white girls what to do because they
are the only ones who will listen to me.
Before mom and dad get home from work
I feed the dog peanut butter
smothered in hot sauce.
I try on all of my mother's brand new
Avon products and apply her red lipstick.
Before bed I eat the toothpaste
instead of brushing my teeth with it.
I dream that I am Michael Jackson.

Roseart

I remember when my friends wore Adidas
And I thought I was dope in my dollar store sneakers
Stevie on the Ipod, Mariah Carey, my god
Hitting high notes that you know could blow speakers
I would go deep and catch a pass, one hand
No grass on the land but they called me moss
All we thought about then is untouchable
Who liked who? Who brought the best Lunchable?
I, on the other hand a little uncomfortable
How everybody Harry and my body so Hobbit?
Damn how it hurt that I wasn't fit for skirts
But how easily my body slipped right into the closet
Hanging on by the thread of my Paco jeans
But still free, swang my legs jumping off them swings
Too happy, could've cracked my head on cement
Blue khakis, turning black as all my secrets
Now the 24 pack of Crayolas turn into Modelos
If you eva wonder bout me been working 24–7
Tryin to face the storm with all the shifting weather
But dude it ain't no Elmer's glue to hold the shit together
I'll admit it, I been bitter, missing glitter and gold stars
Giving masterpieces and treating girls to my Roseart
Feet in a circle, point ya fingers where yo toes are
Run til we outta breath and after just doze off
Then reset, long as it didn't hurt my grades,
Now recess is a 30 minute break unpaid
Hey, we would swallow cartons
Just to see who gulped the hardest
Now I gotta buy the gallon every Sunday
I think I miss the closet just a little bit
Wish I could switch direct deposits for my innocence

I think I miss my mama and my daddy I forget him
And I think about it all every night of every autumn

Kz

I beat my sistas ass foreal this time

and I'm staring
down at her
in awe of my bloody hands

in a twist of her hurt, I wince
too. my anger dissipates like
air out of her lungs.

i never want to see her looking like me / nursing
scars and sunken. Another
brown girl beat bloody. Another
family blown cloudless

broken open
and squinting into
all our gore and pleading.

In another life
I remember our backs tilled
fresh by some overseer // or father
remember shame dragging at our necks.

In another life, I remember she is my only love.

                    sacred trinity

her bruises   my scars

            the same source, really;
            broken black girl Commodity

memory full
of triggers and we
are always aiming.

This Poem for Sugar Hill, Harlem

This poem for Peanut, who robbed Mama and me in our elevator, when I was nine.
He was high on that stuff.
This poem for Squeak Squeak, our chihuahua, who didn't say peep in that elevator when we was being robbed.
Mama said he was a good for nothing little pet, but I ain't stopped loving him.
This poem for Tiff, Peanut's sister.
She was my best friend until that happened.
This poem for Miss Mary up on Amsterdam Ave, who was married to Mr. Leon, the numbers runner.
Every day I went to their candy store, gave them twenty dollars for Grandma's daily news and daily numbers and sometimes Miss Mary would give me a handful of green apple jolly ranchers, if she saw me staring at the display behind the counter too long.
This poem for Grandma Pearl.
The year she hit the numbers for five thousand was like magic.
She paid for Mama and me to take a bus ride to Disney World allllllll the way from Harlem.
It didn't matter it was a bus and we was the only ones who spoke English, cause everybody was so happy to get to the magic kingdom.
Anyhow, Mama's Spanish wasn't half bad, was enough to make a bunch of new friends on that longgggggg ass bus ride.
This poem for Mama who didn't drink a lick of vodka that whole trip.
I wanted to send Miss Mary and Mr. Leon a thank you note for those lucky numbers.
But Mama just sucked her teeth and said:
"Just tell 'em in person when we get back baby girl. Anyhow, you know those numbers ain't legal right?"

This poem for that long ass trip back home to Sugar Hill and our
elevator up on 149th, that I wouldn't ride again for the next seven years.
Every year our neighbor on the first floor, Ms. Janis, asked Mama, "Girl
that chile still walking up all those stairs?" while she shook her head in
disgust.
Eventually Peanut went to jail.
Then Tiff had a baby our junior year of high school.
We stayed friends, I just didn't tell Mama when I went to her family's
place over on Convent.
Her baby looked just like dolls we played with growing up, except cuter.

Rachelle M. Parker

Ode to Walt Whitman
. . . The Housing Project

Thirteen stories pushed through cracks.
Capped with water tanks and smoke stacks.
Insulated from the big, bad world.
My dreams and imagination swirled.
White concrete walls were a blank slate.
Held my name up in bright red paint.

Enough flights of stairs to fly down.
Steps taken two by two until on the ground.
Summer you offered the most fun.
Long days, long kisses from the sun.
Yellow outlines for games with cans.
Part of a day with no set plans.

Maple trees lined our racetrack.
The tar, if you fell, showed no slack.
Jump rope slaps from telephone wire.
No amount of number rocks could tire.
Doting on us kids to show your care.
The ice cream truck's weight you'd bear.

Halls are now dank and dark.
Every kind of crime left its mark.
Silver chain links replaced with black bars.
Scaffolding begins to block the stars.
As brick and mortar swell with fears.
Panes and panes of glass shed tears.

Never daunted by all these things.
Wisely, you still know the heart that sings.

Musty jacket tattered and worn.
At attention and blowing your horn.
Fiercely you continue standing guard.
Over little girls in cowboy boots and leotards.

All water has a perfect memory
and is

to get back to where it was.

—TONI MORRISON

Idrissa Simmonds

Flight

I call to ask my mother the name of the street where we bought the
   suitcases when we left
Brooklyn. A better question would have been how did it feel to be sliced
   from the rib of Pine and
Loring and sent, like a kite, up North. Or tell me what your mother said
   to you in her grand rear
room the night we left, seated on the edge of her bed in her nightgown,
   muted in the low light.
So many bellies in the house. Cacophony of kreyol and Brooklyn buk and
   sweet sweat across the
walls. Did she tell you to follow your husband. Did she tell you anything
   about us. How, above
all, you should keep us anchored to here, where the distance between
   comfort and safety was
measurable by the length of the hallway, the distance from one room to
   the next. The rooms, like
capsules, each with it's own medicine for black kids. Or, tell me what you
   wore on the plane
ride. I only remember what I wore: stockings and mary janes and the pink
   knit pleated skirt. I did
not remember this was your first time flying, a grown woman over thirty,
   and you had never seen
how small the world looked beneath your feet.

What Women Are Made Of

There are many kinds of open
                              —**Audre Lorde, "Coal"**

We are all ventricle, spine, lung, larynx, and gut.
Clavicle and nape, what lies forked in an open palm;

we are follicle and temple. We are ankle, arch,
sole. Pore and rib, pelvis and root

and tongue. We are wishbone and gland and molar
and lobe. We are hippocampus and exposed nerve

and cornea. Areola, pigment, melanin, and nails.
Varicose. Cellulite. Divining rod. Sinew and tissue,

saliva and silt. We are blood and salt, clay and aquifer.
We are breath and flame and stratosphere. Palimpsest

and bibelot and cloisonné fine lines. Marigold, hydrangea,
and dimple. Nightlight, satellite, and stubble. We are

pinnacle, plummet, dark circles, and dark matter.
A constellation of freckles and specters and miracles

and lashes. Both bent and erect, we are all give
and give back. We are volta and girder. Make an incision

in our nectary and Painted Ladies sail forth, riding the back
of a warm wind, plumed with love and things like love.

Crack us down to the marrow, and you may find us full
of cicada husks and sand dollars and salted maple taffy

weary of welding together our daydreams. All sweet tea,
razor blades, carbon, and patchwork quilts of *Good God!*

and *Lord Have Mercy!* Our hands remember how to turn
the earth before we do. Our intestinal fortitude? Cumulonimbus

streaked with saffron light. Our foundation? Not in our limbs
or hips; this comes first as an amen, a hallelujah, a suckling,

swaddled psalm sung at the cosmos' breast. You want to
know what women are made of? Open wide and find out.

french guiana/enigmatic
womyn blues

black girl, french maid, thick rope lips wrapped around future, fortune
between thunder thighs, swol breasts, sassy favorite accountant, colony
in jordan river mississippi pool eyes, your favorite one-night mistake,
wifey fuh real, pussy in a jar, red lipstick engineer, blood on veneer,
blood on canvas, cinnamon-stick blushing, the one who stayed, big belly
gold womb, panther aesthetic, gap teef swallow ya whole lyfe, position
power, queen bitch honor thesis, fetish for the meat of it, the sweetest
meal is the one you have killed yourself, resistance makes my body a
spear, they will still try to eat the knife of me, for the beauty of it, love
how I make em bleed, nails in they skin and they still call me a delicacy,
eat me, eat we, eat us, crack teeth on this skin, sour to the colonizer's
stomach, this is how the world tried to write a biological biography, they
still can't finish, still can't consume completely, won't emancipate what
they can't understand, still think they got some semblance of control,
cackle in they faces, ask black hole questions, they'll call us crazy, what's
a gyal to do?

Safia Elhillo

old wives' tales

spraying perfume on your hair will turn it gray   a black cardamom
seed will cure any ache   white toothpaste will cool a burn   a man will
make your hips big   braiding your hair before bed keeps it from falling
out in the night   caramel removes body hair   wearing   shorts   is
an invitation [men like big-legged girls]   spraying perfume on an open
wound will clean it   wearing your hair loose invites the evil eye & it will
fall out in the night   a pierced nose means you are ready to marry
a small chest means you are not eating enough red meat   walking too
much will shrink you [men like big-legged girls]   castor oil will make
your hair grow back a prayer bound up in leather will protect you from
the evil eye   a prayer dissolved in water   casts a spell

Vespers

*On August 6, 1964, the group Jeune Haiti disembarked at Petite
Rivière de Dame Marie in the south of Haiti, in an attempt to liberate
the country from the terrors of François Duvalier who had dissolved
the Parliament and proclaimed himself president for life. For many
reasons, including the assistance expected from the population that did
not materialize, these young guerilleros were either killed or captured
one by one. —fordi9.com*

When you answer only to one man
there is no place in your mouth for the hard wall
of questions.
When the man is well-spoken, austere, sprawling with power,
you learn to obey each twitch of his face.
You see Baron Samedi
when he smiles at you
and this smile becomes your loa.
He, your president for life, bids you
to cock your elbow
ready your machete
with your free hand
grip the neck of the cretin
on his knees before you—
mangy black dog that he is—
and strike the life from him.
You will do this
again
and again
and again
Until you are a panoply of iron
and clacking teeth and torn fingerbeds.
God by your will

was your prayer every morning,
before the cup of black coffee
and the bowl of labouyi bannann
before the feel of your mother
moving through the room like light
This, strangely, is the image that grips
you as the last dog lies dying,
his red mouth hung open like sunrise.

poem that wrote me into beast in order to be read

samira and aziza nabila awatef and 3adaal isis and ma'at yes ma'at of the 42
laws and ideals we used to live by you of white feather and commandment
who made us taught us of stars and named them named us made nout
and systems of irrigation nile delta source inventors of mead and kohl for
drawing of lapis and woven cloth and harp sinai berber pen and paper we
were winged creatures werent we tell me because i still dream of flight
sometimes i trumpet waiting to be sound i who have made earrings of
arrow reporting now to you of the mythical creatures i dismantled
in order to become the one writing words you are reading tarsal by
metatarsal i disjointed false to be true sometimes i am cell with eyes made
up of five strand DNA quintuple helix amoeba bond i would claim you
as my ancestors thrice but once is honor i am trying to be worthy live
to have learned so much that god made arab to know what it is to be
both black and jew to be arab is to beast in order to be read like scripture
etched calligraphy wooden metal i ask you to marvel at poetry they tried
to make us forget in guantánamo and all unnamed time will ask us of this
time come back again and again while we were out the world has become
image we made in our own image and this is what we hunt now ive caught
my reflection between incisors i beast of no nation who want only to be
read excuse me   now   it is time   to be   fed

Hiwot Adilow

Abandon

Whenever a blk person is senselessly murdered
(and I shiver through the bones at how
smooth it comes, like wind across my cheek,
the bitter truth that waves *whenever*)

I find myself, my Other name, biting at
The Atlantic—I will simply go *Back Home.*
Ethiopia waits for my lips, spitting
My father's name so wrong.

There is blood in the city I was born in
And it trails from one coast to another.
I say *beYesussm* and dream of flight
Wondering where the dying will go.

Can I pull them onto the boat I inherited?
Who is to say *I* will not die running?
Who is to say that the bullet cares
Anything for where I am "from?"

Parcel Map
for the County Assessor

No one talks about gentrified country in-betweens.
The boxing up of hunting and nesting grounds
packaging them into cookie-cutter subdivisions
with snap-on aluminum siding, rowed like bottles of Clorox
on store shelves, HOAs measuring the width of each blade of grass.

Ours was the land of pipe organ roosters, who accordioned
their songs from 4 hours before dawn to 2 hours before dusk.
Of the hunter's pop echo. Of centenarian pines ricocheting warning
to deer families crossing backyards. Of horse farmers
who trotted out onto the road, pranced, twirled, and would let us ride
if our granddaddy's home.

Of grandads who coated the house sunshine yellow for one decade
and peacock turquoise for another, strictly for the joy of it.
Of the matching mailbox and tires half buried and flanking the gravel drive.
Of old men who walked The Road on warring hipbones,
a quarter mile to the first neighbor, then on to the next. Visiting.

That branch in back has overgrown the rusted chainlink knots,
saplings cover the wood plank no longer parabolaed below,
and that path we ran to get to the call of maple syrup biscuits
is as weedy as any forgotten way.

Maybe these readymade, justaddwater houses came
when the old men crossed over. The vigilantes who paced the pavement
checking in, patrolling the woods, when possible
wheezing a belly laugh all over you, when needed
toting a rifle.

Destiny O. Birdsong

400 Heat

I'm most American when I reach for more ketchup
as Shaunae Miller dives across the finish.

I'm blackest when Allyson Felix collapses
on the track, knees up, concealing her last name

and the letters "USA" emblazoned on her chest.
I'm saddest whenever black women are competing

because I never know who to root for,
and I'm arrogant enough to believe my split loyalty

fails them (which makes me more American again).
This is how it feels to be a problem:

hoping that, when a country's cameras are trained
on your back, and you offer the fruited plain

of your body, it's somehow enough to quench
the parched land where all the fathers keep dying.

Each is a breath-song trilling in your blood,
and, perhaps, one day, a grand mal convulsion:

petechiae like pomegranate seeds jeweling your face.
Every race is a transubstantiation of flesh,

just not to gold, nor bronze, nor mythical filigree,
but to the fleeting, nameless moment when a foot

finds the white chalk of a line drawn by someone else.

that mean nothing until after you're dead. Who knows what metals
the gods use to forge victory, which is neither sympathy

nor love, nor more sacred than the foot-fall, its indiscernible blip
magnified for the millions of eyes that never blink

when we're winning, which you too might have missed, although
later, in the dashcam footage, you'll swear you saw it.

Fayise Abrahim

BLACK PRODUCE

no indictment. lines still move

beer. fresh blooms. shorter queue on a rainy afternoon
when many aren't lingering on tv screens & decisions

Kwame says the language of death is a dialect of betrayals

murmurs. shuffling feet. bright lights. lies. won story. one sided

someone else bags your groceries today and
gives you the news and gives you the receipt
and gives you the price

of one story. your story. not your story.

the store's yellow chairs shine here. they are safer in these
halls than us. then us. when us?

tell me what a man said when he is no longer living and bring death to
    all of us

Families stand. lean on each other. lean on themselves. lean away from the
walls placid the aisles. lining the day. prices we pay when they run out of
grocery bags but still have bags for bodies.

registers fall silent. still snicker the coins. worth waiting. for dimes
wonder why the belts move so slow and automatic doors let in cold air

coffee? deli? cook now eat later. eat now cook later. so much can fit
in stores selling routine selling normal. give me normal/the desperation.
his words too slow broadcasting live when hearts already know

handcuffs. many. many hands. whose hands?
what time? who waits outside of ambulance doors?

rewind the story/speak it backwards/see the fear/see the blatant codes
the comments/the visibility of wholes

watch for slippery floors. construct safety
in-between the canned foods and the butcher.
between the pastas and the flowers

safety between contested roads.
you can't read the streets you don't belong to.
and the scanner struggles to digest barcodes today

Mahogany L. Browne

Built for Disaster

Nothing feels certain here, America is tilting again and again and if I close my eyes tightly, it almost feels like 1989. Everything is a choice, depending on the day. If I am feeling insecure:

My mother didn't love me enough to beat her addiction.

And if I am feeling steady, my feet bolted into the earth, my very existence is championed with each breath:

Of course I survived, I was built for all of this disaster.

Yesterday, I was only a fizzle. Today, I write like I'm not. Like I escaped the battlefield with my parts, detached and dragging, a trail of wreckage spilling all my secrets. This is an occupational hazard: to speak in front of a mass of people and pretend the hurt is poetry. It is also a magic trick— to reveal the missing limb while claiming the poetry is healing. Tadaw!

But what if the limb is a whole body, a shaking mother or the earthly father?

For the past three years I have written a manuscript using my parents' love story (a story I wasn't alive to witness and when I was alive it had dimmed to ash) as an easel in which I envision the foundation of family. I interviewed family members. I researched pictures. I recorded my grandmother's voice and transcribed her memories. It enabled me to write the story of my birth. But there are always several sides to the truth. A perspective that wavers when dreams arrive lucid, or sobriety is a slow wind with regret on her mind. I wrote poems that made my existence make sense. I couldn't remember my mother and father together. I had no instructional manual of how love is built. How love sustains. I only remember the aftermath. How the fire of violence can scorch a foundation. In my father's absence, I learned to fear love. To worry of its ability to strangle a black woman until cold. How it could leave a child with only memories of white dust, violent arms, and trauma. I am writing the success of my every breath. I don't know how I got here, living in a blistered city thousands of miles away from my parents. But I do know that everything around me smells like fire and despite the whispers telling me to get ghost, I love.

Nina Angela Mercer

Root Song for Daughter

*Word is I made my womb safe house for insurgent birds, rebels by bloodline
and ready to fly free, peck some heads, one born from flesh. I am mother, not
anybody's piece (ottoman, table, toilet). I wear my heart on top my crown.
And you, my daughter, are meant to soar.*

*But pray your song a river when you sing it. Let it stretch all the way out over
years. Consider the sun's light a road. Touch tree bark. Lean close. Listen.*

1977. DC was still the Chocolate City then. I wore my hair in two
long braids. Me and Mommy wore marigold matching jumpsuits on a
runway in a downtown hotel for the Jewels of Ann school fundraiser.
My mother sewed hers first, then mine to match. I held her hand tight
on the runway in my matching marigold jumpsuit sewn carefully by her
hands. She was fly. Her black mane serious and flipped in the front. Her
lips glazed red brick. Her open-toe wedge sandals.

I watched her for years.

By the late eighties, I was covetous of her gold scarab ring with the
ruby eyes, her black leather pants and jacket, her Fashion Fair lipsticks
and Opium perfume. But there was no hand-holding inside this new
becoming. We took an adversaries' stance. She woke me past midnight,
pulling every secret from under my bed, and from the furthest corner in
my closet, until her borrowed belongings were recovered. I learned there
could be no secrets in my parents' house. My mother knew my stealth from
conception, so that when I lost my virginity she saw through my crocodile
tears and took me to her gynecologist, got me on birth control pills, and
told me, *I don't need to know when you're doing it, but I do need to know that
you are protected.* She did not want grandbabies any time soon. She needed
to know that I was clear about that. She also needed me to know I should
always have my own money, file my own taxes, maintain good credit, and

have my own road to walk. She married her college sweetheart at twenty-two years old and became a mother by the time she was twenty-five. Her world was bound to home and a nine-to-five while my father traveled to Cameroon, Haiti, Trinidad, Paris, Nigeria, and Japan, taking risks he would not have taken, if he were charged with raising me alone.

I admired his wide wings, his flight.

I watched my mother.

And I was certain I would make a mess if I ever had to match her method.

Do remember, pray your road while you walk it. Consider sun's light. Touch river water. Do remember, you were conceived in love.

I became your mother blasting Biggie in the shower of my basement apartment in northeast DC. It was my senior year, Howard University, Chocolate City, still. It was 1994 and I was twenty-one years old. Four years younger than my mother was when she discovered she was pregnant with me. Me and my girls met Luke and Redman on a Potomac River boat ride that never left the dock. The boat was so packed it was unsafe to sail. But we ain't care. Late nights, Snoop and Dre chanted over a booming bass and a game of bones. A box of fresh oranges covered the smell of dank delivered to campus from Cali. We were Freaknik, "Party and Bullshit," the slow crawl and masquerade on Peachtree in Atlanta, and late-night chocolate chip cookies eaten straight out the pan, still hot. We were sunglasses and bare legs in jean shorts, gliding through some righteous haze and Roy Ayers' "Everybody Loves the Sunshine." We were head wraps and Timberlands, Dr. Frances Cress Welsing's *The Isis Papers,* and drumming circles in Malcolm X Park. Free love meant blue lights in some sparsely furnished basement apartment, too much patchouli, and late night analyses of conspiracy theories spawned from *Behold a Pale Horse.* Free love could also mean taking youth from the Shaw neighborhood on weekend field trips, making brown bag lunches in the kitchen of university housing. We studied the variations.

Consider darkest night sky, sing past midnight with windows open, make love often. Lean close to your lover. Live without regret:

I became your mother while listening to Biggie in 1994:

Let me ask you a question, yo.
Yo, would you kill for me?

Some truths only made sense over that boom bap. I only killed myself a little. Not for you. But for the lesson. Coming back into full living was a head trip like none other, and it took too damn long. *Remember that.*

One brother dared to grapple with my mind, listening to poems I penned about revenge sex, "The Man," and revolutionary love—a brazen manifesto of political contradictions and food-flavored skin-tone descriptions; a well-intentioned, make-shift, Black Womanist prayer for becoming a different kind of free. Maybe that's all we ever want—to be heard and seen; a desire so crucial we sometimes fall too hard. He walked me from open mics at Mr. Henry's in Adams Morgan and The Andalusian Dog on U Street to his house, where we'd consider the new language our dreams made placed side by side. And he wrote rhymes. Me and my girls came to his shows. When his song played on the radio, I imagined he was only talking to me. We was too fine then. Our bodies fresh-plucked and pulsing. You, baby girl, got made easily. You were conceived in a love too young for caution. We didn't know about how major record labels get sold, and artists' projects get shelved, and how daycare fees can push culture-keeping young parents into nightmares and fantasy escape routes that risk some time behind iron bars. But we found out. He did. And you found out when you called for him before going to sleep. I never thought I'd survive that hurt. We did though. We grew.

Being a mother meant choosing daughter over dreams made relevant by Hollywood and Billboard charts. We watched it all burn in our living room. Daughter over vows. Daughter over escape routes. Daughter, despite shortness of breath, screams without sound on a night of knife-sharp knowledge—sometimes you gotta change the locks, rendering old keys meaningless, and reclaim home. Sometimes your activism is as local as your bedroom.

Do remember, when deepest night sky comes, sing past midnight with windows open. Welcome every crack in your voice unashamed, and listen close for signs of your fugitive truth. Laugh and be frightening. Laugh and let go.

I wonder how many family secrets are about bold women who did life their own way. I wonder why I had to pass into my thirties before I celebrated the knowledge that I come from a lineage including many single mothers. It's not a new thing, and you are not less than anyone because you were raised by one.

Remember.
Your great-grandmother's grandmother, Clara Irwin, was a single mother in New York City in 1894 and a Black woman. She lived on Grove Street in the Village. Only an intersection remains where her home used to be. I imagine what the Village must have been like at that time—poorly lit at night, roughly paved roads and walkways, if they were paved at all. Small rooms for rent in buildings pressed between warehouses. A confusion of commerce during the day, a blatant lawlessness at night. Clara's mother was enslaved by her father. Her grandmother was born in passage across the Atlantic Ocean from Africa. Clara, born enslaved but free by her 11th year, left her life as a domestic working for a married, white circuit court judge, who forcibly fathered two of her children in Montgomery, Alabama, to come north to New York City with her third child, who had a different father from the other two. She came north to sew and repair costumes for a theatre company. She walked from Grove Street to the theatre at night to drop off and pick up costumes, hoping no one would question a solitary Black woman walking fast. And I imagine she had to leave her young daughter alone in their room with special instructions— *Do not unlock the door for anyone, except the nice lady from upstairs who speaks loudest when night pushes toward dawn. Do not play in the hallway. Do not go out into the street.*

I think of Clara when I'm confronted by the way we pathologize the road of single, Black mothers and their children. I think of Clara with dreams audacious enough to carry her all the way to Manhattan. I think of Clara and her daughter when I measure my love for theatre against the statistics predicting narrow odds for Black women writing and producing plays, especially those without partners. I have roots. When I walk across Grove Street on an August night, leaving a club alone after the DJ rocked my worries 'til they vanished in sweat, I call her name—*Clara Irwin.* I pause under the streetlight, listen close for clues, imagine my feet in her black boots, my possibility wed to her own unique hunger for more. I keep on, ride the D train back uptown to the Bronx, enter the apartment, crack your bedroom door open just to know you are there.

Because daughter

Your presence makes doubts a foolish waste of time. Your smile and sly eyes always seem about to plot a way out of lukewarm happenings for some third-eye epiphany. You on that new conjure. You don't ever compromise your truth, or the way you heavy-handed with the spices and in your own defense. A fighter. Be all of that. Make your own beats. Write your own rhymes. Learn the science of healing with plants. Don't court fear, and if you ever find that tight space, breathe through it. Feel the shift that comes with knowing your song in the world. It is far more than any politicians' posturing, beyond the conspiracy theory that nags your mind, telling you we all pawns. You better than any mass media prediction of who and how you be. Live. Be the antidote to wayward group think. Wear your hair wild. Paint it any color, if that pleases you. Be your own kind of sweet that yields to your own volition. Never make yourself small for nobody's comfort. There is a time for anger, rage, patience, love, stillness. Don't make marriage your priority. Join your own self on the bridge. Watch it all go by. Daughter, be your whole self. Travel far. Don't let this country hold you. Laugh loud. Play your music that way, too. And always eat your steamed Chesapeake blue crabs without the help of metal tools. Dump a bushel on newspaper with fresh sweet corn on the cob and red potatoes. Drink your whiskey neat, if you drink it. Take long walks through the city, wherever you live. This is the only way to know your people and where you at. Be a seeker. Never let any mothering you may do for others be more prized than your heart's song for itself. Start there, and when your head feels too difficult to carry, remember this:

Take honey to the river on a clear day. Be sure to taste the honey before you turn the top down

toward the water, and pour slowly as you pray. Let your prayer be song.
Sit near the river after.
Witness the sun's light making a road across the river.

Be sure to taste the honey again before you go.

And always clean yourself with nine pennies at the gates of the cemetery.
Always cover your head when the wind whips strong. And keep a cool
center, even when your passions run hot.

Take molasses to the ocean, and a blanket large enough to spread your
tarot cards out, and still have room for fresh pineapple, or watermelon,
sketchbook, many colored pens. Pour the molasses out slow as you pray.
Take your body into the water. Jump the waves.

And always clean yourself with nine pennies at the gates of the cemetery.
Always cover your head when the wind whips strong.

Touch tree bark when you speak of the mothers who came before us.
Touch tree bark. Lean close. Listen. You have roots.

Remember.

come celebrate
with me that everyday

something
has tried
to kill me
and has
failed.

—LUCILLE CLIFTON

Rio Cortez

WHAT BEGETS WHAT BEGETS

Everything is a ring. I am working on a belief
that starts like that: everything
is a ring, not symmetrical, it has
the illusion of progress

*

I woke up sad so all day long I tried
to make the world sad around me

*

I heard in a movie once that hurt people
hurt people. Now I always say that
when I am comforting sad friends.
I curve the ring so not even I can see it
how it winds right back to itself, loops
right around me when I think
it must be going

I say to myself: look at this sad fool

*

I am always explaining myself to my lover
I say to him: there are two kinds
of knowing. Some knowing is as close
as my own palm, I don't even know
I know it. I love my mother & my mother
loves me. Other knowing gets pushed
beneath

*

Beauty always strikes me when I consider it's going & am hurt by it
how now light enters through the curtains at dusk & I find it beautiful
because it is about to change

*

One layer of that knowing I mentioned, is of the self.
Isn't it like that for everyone. Sometimes
the ring comes round & I feel I don't deserve a thing.
Then I do the work of knowing. I see myself
reflected in the bathroom mirror, it's been a long
day & I am alone, my hair pulled into a tight chignon
& I know better by looking at me next to nothing, compared
to nothing & I say thanks to someone out there

Nabila Lovelace

For Songs and Contests

Let him bow down to me! I am the greater king, . . . the greater man.
—**The Iliad**

This is how
I shed the house:
one boy's broken
cheek after
another. I slapbox
and my hands
are the quickest.
Slapboxing,
the kind of fight
that does not
require reason.
Except. I want
a name. (Sound
familiar?) I
am in proximity
to named
men. In this way
I am any
daughter. Once
I knew a man
who fought
a river,
& kept
both hands. Once
I was called
Anwar's little
cousin.
Once, I didn't have

a name
at all. Who are you
if not boy
and brazen?
A heavy *thwack*
across a boy's face,
and I'm first
of my
name.

Porsha O.

SERENA

raise up the black girl
pay homage to beads that jangle when her braids swing
homage to her swing
and the grunt that creeps from between her lips
praise the shout
and the worship
homage to her racket and how it
        stands
        by her
        like a
        staff
        parting
        a sea
raise up her body
and the apologies that go unheard, for being full
raise up the thighs and their defiance to separate
water, spilling
from underneath a yellow tennis dress.
praise the stolen tennis balls
and practice on courts covered in glass
where god learned to pray
praise the speed gained and the bullets dodged
hold up her survival
how death never comes even though the reaper is sowing
hold up her rage
how it be a shield
how it crouch out like a tiger
to smash a racquet
to curse an ump
to break a tie
raise up taquanda and the sass that only comes from a girl who is black

hold up compton
how she keeps it twinkling between her teeth like a razor blade
in case of need to slice a ref who makes a bad call during game point
praise game point and how it is hers
praise the bad call and how it doesn't stop the worship
raise up whole stadiums who heckle the player
who make a nigger of the father
and an enemy out of their countrymen
hold up the white women who make a spectacle of her figure
and the white women who figure she shouldn't play this sport
praise the salty white girl tears
for it taste like redemption
taste like a dream
hold up the dream
and the women who do the dreaming
hold up the trophy
and the gold
hold up the god
and the girl
who dances
who sings
who plays
who swings and grunts and wins
hold her up
praise her
amen

Angel Nafis

Ghazal for Becoming Your Own Country

After Rachel Eliza Griffiths, "Self Stones Country Series"

Know what the almostgone dandelion knows. Piece by piece
the body prayers home. Its whole head a veil. The wind blown bride.

When all the mothers go gone frame the portraits. Wood spoon over boiling
pot, test the milk on your own wrist. You a soil, sand, and mud grown bride.

If you miss your stop. Or lose love. If even the medicine hurts too.
Even when your sideeye,your face stank, still, your heart moans *bride*.

Fuck the fog back off the mirror. Trust the road is your name. Ride
your moon hide through the pitch black. Gotsta be your own bride.

Burn the honey. Write the letters. What address could hold you?
Nectar arms, nectar hands. Old tire sound against the gravel. Baritone bride.

Goodest grief is an orchard you know. But you have not been killed once.
Angel, put that on everything. Self. Country. Stone. Bride.

79th be the catwalk.

Tyra Banks ain't got shit,
taxes just hit. folks
strut. here is the timber
of our land. we give
the breeze a new cover. girl
some dude with a camera said he could
buy my walk, plus interest
my face. ain't enough
to want my body too. move
like i got somewhere to be. round
here home ain't much of america's
model. my landlord
said i walk like money,
a stain/finesse. examination
is extermination. what was
a short cut is now a safe word
kept for cutting. or just in case
some fool thinks a south side stomp
sweet. commercial. commissary is
a blk girl's stride. to the bus
be blk boiis who grab
their dickies. gucci belt gang
expect me to hold they strap. loose
square sellers all off theirs,
ready to lick or hit one.
they think the bus'll wait for me
but someone else ready to take my spot.
like the white man's hunt ain't my job too. like
they ain't got somewhere to be too. like
we ain't in a hurry to go
someplace where we can just walk.

Thiahera Nurse

Some Girls Survive
on Their Sorcery Alone

I got a stank ass attitude
because you tried to kill me.
           Still, I am the baddest bitch in here.

Diamond yoni. Carbon-based funk & it's everywhere.
Video-vixen bad. Thick with the stuff my mama gave me,
her mama gave her. It's cyclical, this survival. My gap-toothed gait bending
the corner. Bow-legged Athena, if this story needed a white goddess to exist.
Let me compare myself to my black ass self:

a stillborn summer=roadkill=every deer gnawed through= peepholes
    where my breasts should be

How easy it is to eat through the faces
of black girls with your weapons.
A flesh that don't crack
and yet_____.

                              Here I am. My bottom lip split down
                              the middle. You save the fat you want
                              for yourselves. Your daughters pickle my
                              mouth in a jar they keep on the nightstand.

What did slavery do to y'all
to make you treat me this way?
I almost wonder & then I am
distracted by my own brilliance.

Pink lotion slides down the side of my neck,
I'm sweating—running hard, fast, and away from elegy.

*If I die in this jail cell no, I did not kill myself. If I die in this jail cell no, I
did not kill myself.
If I die in this jail cell no, I did not kill myself. If I die in this jail cell no, I
did not kill myself.*

For **Sandra Bland Aiyana Mo'nay Stanley-Jones Renisha McBride
Reese Walker**
Tarika Wilson Kathryn Johnston Shereese Francis Korryn Gaines
and 'nem.
[The understood, implicit et cetera of this list.]

I am trying to mend the impossible wound and I seal it
in cocoa butter. I'm blasting Lil' Kim in the rain. So much
coconut oil on me, the bullets miss. I'm slick as fuck.
You mad you can still smell me breathing from here?

Yesenia Montilla

It's a Miracle

For Denice & Mo & Christina

how my city dies each winter
the trees as bare & raw
as a damn heartbreak
& in the news my president, black
& crying, talking about gun control
on the same day that Matthew's
poem showed up in my mailbox.
& how I couldn't imagine
the words kevlar & children
in back to back stanzas. & how
this just reminds me of '93 when
I saw my first dead body, outside
the bodega. It sported blue Nike's
that looked iridescent like those
fish that camouflage themselves
against the dark ocean. & how her face
looked only eight years old, maybe
ten & how someone's second
amendment right seems to only
leave a trail of children's bodies
& brown bodies. & how some
days I am afraid of stepping out
the house or of whether my lover
brown & beautiful will make it home
& I can't write anymore about death
yet it's all I know. & how tonight
the sky will be all kinds of colors
against the iciness of humanity & isn't
it a miracle that we haven't killed

every last one of us yet? A miracle
that there are still those among us
who sit & wait   hoping for spring—

nonae

creation story after Safia Elhillo

in the beginning was Goddess
                    and Goddess was all
        lips
legs
                life
    laughter

on the seventh day Goddess made trans girls
and the freshly birthed oceans made
the first wave

stretched their salty fingers to get the girls' attention
to tickle the girls' feet with their gentle touch then fall back again
the girls laughed

and their laughter blessed all of the young and dewy world

when the sun heard she blushed red
held girls in her golden light until Goddess
said the day was done

then the stars came
their glitter glowed bright
as trans girls traced them with curious fingers
laughter on their tongues
like goddess made them
like her image

this is our creation story

sister girl take off your heels

land of tgirls and honey

land of the good lesbian sun

land of glow and glittering stars

land of brown girls and laughter

land of golden light and flirting waters

land of the blush and wave

Goddess bless the blush and wave

like She willed this awkward flirtation
and so it will beautifully be

i pledge myself to Her blush and wave
to Her glitter and glow

i pledge myself to no thing that does not love me
                        because what holy thing would hate anyone
                        with Goddess' fingerprints on her skin?

i choose my girlfriend's fingerprints
all over my good brown skin
i pledge myself to my sister girls
to their crooked and brilliant smiles

i choose the reddening blush that blooms on my lesbian cheeks
and the golden light that brown girl cuddling makes of me

i choose holding hands in the daytime
i choose kissing in the daytime
i pledge myself to sex in the daytime

to threesomes with my girlfriend and the blushing sun

i choose holding and being held by bodies
                                        that won't bruise me

i choose soft skin
i choose lips
i choose legs
i choose *alive*

i choose laughter
when we laugh   i swear

Goddess sprouts wings

I want to look happily forward.
I want to be optimistic.
I want to have a dream. I
want to live in jubilee.
I want my
daughters to feel
that they have the power
to at least try to change
things, even in

a world that resists

change with more strength
than they have.

—EDWIDGE DANTICAT

Mahogany L. Browne

We Are All God's

An erasure poem of Frank Ocean's essay following Orlando's Massacre

waves

hair = important (handwritten)

after hebru brantley

Black boy oceanic, a baby
boar bristle brush in your back
pocket, some might confuse it
for a weapon

but you use it to turn solid to liquid
when you pull out your boar
bristle brush, bullets turn
to heavy rain

when you rub
your boar bristle
brush across a pig's pale nose
he melts into a puddle
of blue

you step out
the barber's chair
with 360-degree waves
you wear the atlantic like a crown
all our ancient bones brushed smooth

all day you tend the waters, reach for the brush
for a quick touch-up in the tinted window
of a car

tie it up in black silk
for safekeeping, the way God
wraps his waves in the night sky

each morning you rewrite history
on your scalp

in your version, no one
drowns

Sway

Dear Black girl,

You mispronounced wonder
You hand-me-down strange fruit
You bending-tree-splintered-and-spray rooted life
You stately-pour-mansion mouth with the stars falling out
You grip, grab, and growl
You hold on, stuck black
You surviving scorched temple
Sway.

You bob-head, battle-rap body, and graffiti tongue
causing cacophonies
You harmony and hip-hop booty
Legs
Be standing
Be flyy
Be gathered razor smile and raging
fists
bulging in back pockets for the long walk home
Be ready
Be two to the body and one to the face
Be kicking, screaming
Be
calling all your pieces back
Be love
Be remembering how
You be Black woman
So
been know how
Since mama taught you how to make a braid

and break bread with other Amazons
Gurl,
sway.

You balmy coil beauty making raucous with your hair
You knotted brown black
You dark meat
You volcanic laugh
Say, I own myself
Say, I validate me and birth gods
Raised yo mama and yo mama's mama
ain't nothing but a mammy
taught you everything you know good
O anyhow
Gospel
O hallelujah
Praise
Black girl . . . sway.
Even when your bones hurt
When they make wilt out of your name
Try and blow out your flame
You be bigger
Show 'em you got that ether
Make 'em burn slow
You be inferno,
be progressive
Be fan, clap, and snap
This shit is magic—you'd have to be a Black girl to understand
Show 'em how it all got started
How the bricks got laid
That this is what happens when the ink spills
When your ancestors dance your worth awake.

Dear Black girl,
Sway.
Swoon.
WOOSH!

Invocation

After Aracelis Girmay, Arati Warrier, and Angel Nafis

you were once teenage purveyor of the white girl gospel—zealous pupil
of the hot comb, of oily neck and folded ear, but before that, you were
young. you were asked questions about your dead father and your hair.
your first conversation with god, faithless. child of the singing forehead.
child of the frustrated wrist. your mother yelled because you fell asleep
on your aunt's pillows and now the whole couch smells of you. child
of amorous pomade. everyone can tell where you've been. even bus
windows remember your name. child of the curl that stole the wind's
fury. how could everything about you not be bursting? child of the
busted chongo. child of the broken brush. splitting anything weak in
half while still blushing for a gentle hand. you are your own lesson in
commitment. child of royalty, of the silk scarf before bed. defender from
the cotton resurrected each night to steal you back, every pillowcase a
looming field of ghosts. child of the rained out funeral. child of grocery
bag protection. at age twelve, washing your own hair is your first act of
humility. listening to your blackness, your first mode of resistance. child
of the eloquent scalp, which negotiations did you lose today? how many
times did you lift your hands in ceremony to unravel and partition?
tell us how you learned to fix, fluff, and plait; to wind and plow. how
you were late for class and work doing so. how you skipped breakfast.
how you tended. how you greeted a new ancestor in the mirror and
let their moans trickle and slither down the length of you. how each
strand circles back to its own beginning. child of inheritance, rejecting
gravity & its theorems. the eternal resilience. when the weather catches
you unprepared, you curse each raindrop undoing your labor with
its disrespectful weight; but unlike anything else in the world, when
smothered in water, submerged in a substance thick enough to kill you,
nearly drowned and gasping—you rise, and refusing invisibility, grow to
the size all benevolent gods are.

The Etymology of "CHUUCH!"

chuuch/church

[pronounced without the "r." the "r" is the hump on our backs. too much to weigh/wait. imagine replacing the "r" with "u." the cupping is softer. all the things it holds. it often sounds like "ahh." round and complete. it all comes together. like home.]

1. from the renowned *amen!* meaning *let it be.* or *so it is.* or so may have it. and take into agreement. this the stamp. the let it be said and sold. the solidarity screaming from the stem of our spouts. this is the *yes.*

2. used in positions of *incognegro.* the screech beyond the never lands of our blocks. posted and protecting. remember the code. often known as *i peep game.* or the never ending *i'm on it bro.* closing the deal. the celebration of *i see you.* welcome to my memory for another day. let the house of our bodies be grateful. for our sacrifices have not killed us. yet.

3. said like a vaccine. the awkwardness dancing on your lip before your words fall and ruin the show. this can also be the broken promise. the text you know you won't reply to. the person you drag your heart for with no supplies left to clean. this is sometimes the last stake. the call of *i don't understand, but imma figure this shit out.* the choir is singing and you can't understand anything sang. you sing. for the house is still bouncing. ace boom cooling.

4. this is not to be confused with *sending off.* it's the most honest thing we are unsure of. for every house is not covered. so we cover our prayer with a *this is it. this is real* and our lives. we do not *agree* to this condition of our wellbeing. blast and break our cinderblocks like tambourines. we weave the stories together. thank and talk through our teeth. for *we know. we understand.* we light the sky. shake up with god and find the move. keep the key. keep it pushing.

The Cut Up

After Janelle Monaé

we eat wangs and throw   dem bones on da ground
Shout when we want how we want   holy ghost
hand out my pocket   hit me three times
pigfoot   and a bottle of beer   we
jukejointsouthernbaptist   call every brown drank
whiskey   every grape drank purple   and
every spade   a gotdamned pa'tok   we put That
on everything we love   we strap
M-16s over   our shoulder so you   know
that we   like the wutang clan   ain't nothing
to fuck wit   and we laugh   oh when we laugh
we laugh   loud   loud enough for the ancestors
to catch the rhythm   and all over you
You at the next table with your breadsticks getting cold.
we run a lapclaplaydown   jumpinplacescreamwheeze
all to catch that laugh   and get it all   the way out   like all the joy
clogged up   from the day   let it bust through   windpipes
all at once   bust loose like the first bits   of day
with a mouth full of   sharpened teeth.

Acknowledgments

Kemi Alabi: "Mr. Hotep Says #BlackLivesMatter and He'd Kill a Dyke" published in *Apogee Journal*, Issue 8 (2016). "At H&M, When Another Black Girl Asks If I Work Here" published in *Kweli Journal* (June 2017).

Ariana Brown: "Invocation" published in *HEArt Online*, April 2016. "Supremacy" published in *Muzzle*, June 2017. "A Brief Life" published in *Apricity Magazine*, January 2017.

Athena Dixon: "Chick" published in *pluck! The Journal of Affrilacian Arts and Culture*, Issue 1. "Chick" and "Boxes of Andromeda" published in *No God In This Room* (Winged City Press, 2018).

Niki Herd: "Blue Magic" published in *The Feminist Wire*, Winter 2013.

Alexis Smithers: "The Holy Theatre" published in *The Shade Journal* (Summer 2017).

Bianca Lynne Spriggs: "What Women Are Made Of" published in *Call Her By Her Name* (NUP, 2016); and in *Circe's Lament: Wild Women Poetry Anthology* (Accents Publishing, 2016).

Nikki Wallschlaeger: "This Body Keeps the Keys" published in *Apogee Journal*, Issue 7 (2016). "Sonnet 47" published in *Crawlspace* (Bloof Books, 2017).

Ajanae Dawkins: "Pulling Teeth and Answers Before Dying" published in *Gramma*.

Angel Nafis: "Ghazal for Becoming Your Own Country" published in *Poetry* (November 2016).

Camonghne Felix: "Meat" published in *The Rumpus*, and filmed by Def Poetry.

Destiny O. Birdsong: "400 Heat" published as "The 400-Meter Heat" in   213
Southern Quarterly, issue 55.1 (Fall 2017).

Elizabeth Acevedo: "La Negra Takes Medusa to the Hair Salon"
published in *The Rumpus*, March 2016. "Mami Came To This Country
as a Nanny" published in *Puerto Del Sol,* September 2015. "Cuero"
excerpted from *The Poet X (*Harper Collins, 2018).

E'mon Lauren: "79th be the Catwalk." and "The Etymology of
"CHUUCH!" published in *COMMANDO* (Haymarket Books, 2017).

Eve L. Ewing: "why you cannot touch my hair" published in *HEArt
Journal,* April 2016, and *Electric Arches* (Haymarket Books,
2017). "what I mean when I say I'm sharpening my oyster knife"
published by the Poetry Society of America and in *Electric Arches.*

Hiwot Adilow: "Abandon" published in *The Black Voice,* October 2015.

Mariahadessa Ekere Tallie: "Homage to my Breasts" published in *The
Wide Shore,* Issue 3, January 2016.

Marwa Helal: "poem that wrote me into beast in order to be read"
published in *BOMB Magazine,* issue 137, September 2016.

Morgan Parker: "Magical Negro #217: Diana Ross Finishing a Rib in
Alabama, 1990s" published in *Lenny.* "Magical Negro #607: Gladys
Knight on the 200th Episode of *The Jeffersons*" published in *Electric
Literature,* issue 200.3. "Magical Negro #80: Brooklyn" published on
Buzzfeed.

Naomi Extra: "Girdle" published in *Sporklet 7* and "My Favorite
Things" published in *Day One,* issue 2.41.

Safia Elhillo: "old wives' tales," "self-portrait with dirty hair," and "self-
portrait with the question of race," published in *The January Children*
(University of Nebraska Press, 2017).

Acknowledgments

Simone Savannah: "beautiful black queen" was first published in *Voicemail Poems*, October 2016.

Teri Ellen Cross Davis: "Piece," from *Haint*, reprinted by permission of Gival Press; published as "A Piece of Tail" in *Tempu Tupu!/walking Naked: Africana Women's Poetic Self-portrait* (Africa World Press, 2007); and in *Beltway Poetry Quarterly* 5, no 3 (Summer 2004).

Yesenia Montilla: "It's a Miracle" published in *African Voices*, July 2016.

About the Authors

Contributors

Curtis Bryant

MAHOGANY L. BROWNE

Mahogany L. Browne is a writer, organizer, and educator. Currently the artistic director of Urban Word NYC, Browne has received literary fellowships from Air Serenbe, Cave Canem, Poets House, and Rauschenberg. She hosts/curates the Nuyorican Poets Cafe Friday Night Slam Series and is the author of *Black Girl Magic* (Roaring Brook/ Macmillan), *Kissing Caskets* (Yes Yes Books), *Dear Twitter* (Penmanship Books) and the out of print titles *Smudge* (Button Poetry) and *Redbone* (Willow Book), which was nominated for an NAACP Image award.

Ron Filio

IDRISSA SIMMONDS

Idrissa Simmonds grew up in Vancouver, British Columbia, with roots in Brooklyn, Haiti, and Jamaica. Winner of the 2013 Crab Creek Review Poetry Prize, she has been a finalist for the Commonwealth Short Story Award and a New York Foundation for the Arts Grant in poetry. Her work has most recently appeared in *Black Renaissance Noire, James Franco Review, Fourteen Hills Press, Room* magazine, and elsewhere. She has led writing workshops for a range of communities through the New York Writers Coalition and curates the literary salon Brunch and Word. Her work as an educator and facilitator focuses on amplifying the voices and talents of educators whose identities and backgrounds are underrepresented in senior leadership roles. She has been the recipient of fellowships and residencies from Hedgebrook, the Bread Loaf Writers Conference, Poets House, and VONA/Voices. She is an MFA candidate in fiction at Warren Wilson College and is at work on her first novel.

Zoe Rain

JAMILA WOODS

Jamila Woods is a poet, singer-songwriter, and educator from Chicago, Illinois. A recipient of the 2015 Ruth Lilly and Dorothy Sargent Rosenberg Poetry Fellowship, her poetry has been published by the Poetry Foundation, Haymarket Books, and Third World Press. She currently works as associate artistic director of the nonprofit organization Young Chicago Authors, where she teaches poetry to Chicago youth and helps organize Louder Than A Bomb, the largest youth poetry festival in the world. As a singer-songwriter, she has collaborated with Chance The Rapper and Macklemore, and toured supporting Corinne Bailey Rae. She also served as music consultant for the web series *Brown Girls*. Her critically acclaimed debut album, *HEAVN*, was rereleased via JagJaguwar Records and Closed Sessions in 2017.

Contributors

FAYISE ABRAHIM is a time-traveling memoirist, poet, and science-fiction writer. Raised in rural Minnesota by a family of East African refugees, factory workers, and farmers, her writing explores rural life, Ethio-futurisms, Oromo traditionalism, and Blackness. Fayise is a 2018 CURA Neighborhood Arts Initiative Grantee, a 2017 Intermedia Arts VERVE Spoken Word Fellow, and a 2016 Emerging Writer with the Givens Foundation for African American Literature.

ELIZABETH ACEVEDO holds a BA in performing arts from George Washington University and an MFA in creative writing from the University of Maryland. She is a National Poetry Slam Champion and has received fellowships from Cave Canem, CantoMundo, and the Callaloo Writer's Workshop. She is the author of *Beastgirl & Other Origin Myths* (YesYes Books, 2016) and her debut novel, *The Poet X* (HarperCollins, 2018).

HIWOT ADILOW is an Ethiopian American poet from Philadelphia. She is the author of *In The House of My Father* (Two Sylvias Press, 2018), winner of the 2017 Two Sylvias chapbook prize. Her poems have been published in *The Offing*, *Nepantla*, *Winter Tangerine*, and elsewhere.

KEMI ALABI is a writer, editor, and facilitator. Their poetry and essays appear in *Catapult*, *Winter Tangerine*, *Apogee Journal*, the *Guardian*, and elsewhere. As editorial manager of the nonprofit organization Forward Together, they coordinate Echoing Ida, a home for Black women and nonbinary writers. They live in Chicago.

JUSTICE AMEER is a Black trans woman poet based in Providence, RI. Xe is a Pink Door Fellow and a three-time semifinalist at the national college slam, CUPSI. Xe is the 2017 Providence Grand Slam Champion and a 2017 FEM Slam Champion. Xyr work is a practice in becoming unapologetic and unafraid, writing in dedication to xyr community and xyr name. You can find xyr work on Glass Poetry Press and wusgood.

DESTINY O. BIRDSONG is a poet and essayist whose poems have appeared or are forthcoming in *African American Review*, *Indiana Review*, *Muzzle*, *Bettering American Poetry Volume II*, *Split This Rock's Poem of the Week*, and elsewhere. Her critical work recently appeared in *The Cambridge Companion to Transnational American Literature*. Destiny has received fellowships from Cave Canem, Callaloo, and Jack Jones Literary Arts, and residencies from Pink Door, the Ragdale Foundation, and the MacDowell Colony.

ARIANA BROWN is a Black Mexican American poet from San Antonio, Texas, with a BA in African Diaspora studies and Mexican American studies. She is the recipient of two Academy of American Poets Prizes, a 2014 national collegiate poetry slam champion, and is currently working on her first manuscript.

RIO CORTEZ is a graduate of Sarah Lawrence College and the MFA program at NYU. Her manuscript, *I Have Learned to Define a Field as a Space Between Mountains*, was selected by Ross Gay as the winner of the inaugural Toi Derricotte & Cornelius Eady Chapbook Prize and is available from Jai-Alai Books. More info: riocortez.com.

TERI ELLEN CROSS DAVIS is the author of *Haint*, winner of the 2017 Ohioana Book Award for poetry, a Cave Canem fellow, and a member of the Black Ladies Brunch Collective (BLBC). She is the poetry coordinator for the Folger Shakespeare Library and lives in Maryland with her husband, the poet Hayes Davis, and their two children.

AJANAE DAWKINS is a Michigan and New York native. She has been published in *undr_scr review*, *the blueshift journal*, and *word riot*. She is a poetry editor for wusgood.black and a teaching artist. The only thing she believes in more than poems is the transformative power of Christ.

ATHENA DIXON is a poet and essayist and is founder and editor in chief of *Linden Avenue Literary Journal*. Her work has appeared in *Narratively*, *Great Lakes Review*, *The Rising Phoenix Review*, *For Harriet*, and *pluck!*, among others. Her chapbook, *No God In This Room*, is forthcoming from Winged City Press, 2018. Athena is a 2017 Callaloo Fellow and has been twice nominated for the Pushcart Prize as well as Best of the Net. Additionally, she has been a speaker at AWP (2013) and HippoCamp (2016, 2017, 2018). She earned her MFA from Queens University of Charlotte. A native of northeast Ohio, she now resides in Philadelphia.

Nicholas Nichols

SAFIA ELHILLO is the author of *The January Children* (University of Nebraska Press, 2017), which received the Sillerman First Book Prize for African Poets. Sudanese by way of Washington, DC, she is a Cave Canem fellow and holds an MFA in poetry from the New School.

EVE L. EWING is a Chicago-born poet, essayist, and sociologist. She is the author of *Electric Arches* (Haymarket Books, 2017) and *Ghosts in the Schoolyard: Racism and School Closings on Chicago's South Side* (University of Chicago Press, 2018). Her work has appeared in the *New York Times*, the *New Yorker*, *Atlantic*, the *Washington Post*, and many other venues.

NAOMI EXTRA is a freelance writer, poet, and doctoral candidate in American studies at Rutgers University–Newark. In both her creative and scholarly work, she explores the themes of agency and pleasure in the lives of Black women and girls. Her writing can be found in *Lenny Letter*, *Bitch*, *Ms.* blog, *Apogee Journal*, the *Paterson Literary Review*, and elsewhere.

CAMONGHNE FELIX, MA, has received fellowships from Cave Canem, Callaloo, and Poets House and is an alumnus of the NYU Arts Politics MA program and the Bard MFA program. The 2012 Pushcart Prize nominee is the author of the chapbook *Yolk*, was recently listed by Black Youth Project as a "Black Girl from the Future You Should Know," and has been published in various outlets, including *Poetry*, Academy of American Poets, *Buzzfeed Reader*, *Teen Vogue*, PEN America, *The Offing*, and *The Shallow Ends*. Her debut collection of poems, *Build Yourself a Boat*, was a 2017 University of Wisconsin Press Brittingham and Pollak Prize finalist, was shortlisted for the 2017 Fordham University Poets Out Loud prize, and is forthcoming from Haymarket Books in 2019.

ARACELIS GIRMAY is the author of the collage-based picture book *changing, changing* and the poetry collections *Teeth*, *Kingdom Animalia*, and *the black maria*. She has received fellowships from the NEA and from the Cave Canem, Jerome, and Whiting foundations. Aracelis is on the faculty of Hampshire College's School for Interdisciplinary Arts. She lives in Brooklyn with her family.

WHITNEY GREENAWAY is a Caribbean author whose work deftly dissects societal structure, introducing conversations of pride, classism, and patriarchy to cultures where these injustices are often deemed acceptable. Whitney has performed across North America and the West Indies, and has also facilitated workshops using writing as a tool for demystifying shame and hierarchies perpetuated by cultural expectations. She is the author of the chapbook *Reasons I Will Leave My Lover*, and her writings have been featured in *pluck!*

THABISILE GRIFFIN is from the West Side of Chicago. A doctoral candidate and historian at UCLA, she researches eighteenth-century Black Caribbean resistance against empire and has published in the *Boston Review* in response to "Black Study, Black Struggle." Thabisile is also a violinist, performance artist, and organizer, cofounding The Undercommons freedom school based in Los Angeles. Her poetry was recently featured as a solo track on Elzhi's album *Lead Poison*, entitled "The Turning Point."

ALYSIA NICOLE HARRIS is a PhD candidate in linguistics at Yale University. Winner of the 2014 and 2015 Stephen Dunn Poetry Prizes, Alysia was selected for publication in *Best New Poets 2015*. Her chapbook *How Much We Must Have Looked Like Stars to Stars* (Finishing Line Press) won the 2015 New Women's Voices Series Contest. She lives in ATL.

MARWA HELAL is the author of the forthcoming *Invasive species* (Nightboat Books, 2019) and winner of *BOMB Magazine*'s 2016 Poetry Prize. She is a fellow of Brooklyn Poets, Cave Canem, and Poets House. She received her MFA in creative writing from The New School.

DESTINY HEMPHILL is a poet and healer based in Durham, North Carolina. She is a 2017 Callaloo Fellow and 2016 Amiri Baraka Scholar at Naropa University's Summer Writing Program. Her work has appeared in *Scalawag, Narrative Northeast*, and *Button Poetry*.

NIKI HERD's poems have been nominated twice for a Pushcart Prize and have appeared in several journals and anthologies, including *Lit Hub, North American Review, The Feminist Wire, Feminist Formations, Split This Rock, The Ringing Ear: Black Poets Lean South*, and *Resisting Arrest: Poems to Stretch the Sky*. Her debut collection, *The Language of Shedding Skin*, was published as part of Main Street Rag's Editor's Select Series. She lives in Houston.

EBONI HOGAN is a Brooklyn-based multi-disciplinary artist who has performed in over sixty-five US cities, as well as internationally in Ghana, Germany, and Austria. She is the 2012 Women of the World Poetry Slam Champion, a Pushcart Prize nominee, and a two-time representative of the Nuyorican Slam Team. Her plays *Foreign Bodies* and *30,000 Teeth* were featured at the National Black Theater of Harlem, the Living Theater, and in the Culture Project's Women Center Stage Festival.

JP HOWARD is the author of *SAY/MIRROR* (The Operating System, 2016), which was a finalist for the Lambda Literary Award. She is the recipient of a 2016 Lambda Literary Emerging Writer Award and has received fellowships and grants from Cave Canem, VONA, and Lambda Literary. JP curates the Women Writers in Bloom Poetry Salon in NYC.

Sherridon Poyer

CANDICE ILOH is a first-generation Nigerian American writer and teaching artist residing in Brooklyn, NY, whose writing has appeared in *Fjords Review*, The Grio, *For Harriet*, Blavity, *No Dear Magazine*, *Glass Poetry Journal*, *Puerto Del Sol*, and elsewhere. She is a recipient of fellowships from VONA, Home School via Lambda Literary fellowship, as well as a Rhode Island Writers Colony Writer-in-Residence alum. She holds an MFA in writing for young people, concentrating in verse, from Lesley University, where she completed her forthcoming young adult novel in verse. She is a 2018 Hi-ARTS Critical Breaks artist residency recipient where she debuted her one-woman show, *ADA: ON STAGE.*

RA MALIKA IMHOTEP is a Black feminist writer/root worker from Atlanta, Georgia, currently pursuing a doctoral degree in African American and African diaspora studies at the University of California, Berkeley. Her thinking engages black femme performance aesthetics and cultural production throughout the Black Diaspora. Her creative praxis is invested in a textual and performative enjoyment of undisciplined movement, the historical present, Black obscenities, Black spiritual practices, and other blackityblk happenings.

RACHEL "RAYCH" JACKSON is a Chicago native who currently teaches fourth grade in the Chicago public school system. In addition to an educator, Rachel is also a poet and playwright. She is the 2017 National Underground Poetry Individual Competition (NUPIC) Champion. Rachel is working on her first book and proudly loves every episode of *Bob's Burgers*.

BRITTENEY BLACK ROSE KAPRI is a teaching artist, writer, performance poet, and playwright based out of Chicago. Currently she is an alumna turned teaching artist fellow at Young Chicago Authors. She is a staff member and writer for Black Nerd Problems as well as the Pink Door Women's Writing Retreat. She has been published in *Poetry, Vinyl Poetry and Prose, Day One, Seven Scribes*, and *Kinfolks Quarterly*. She is a 2015 Rona Jaffe Writers Award Recipient. Her forthcoming book *Black Queer Hoe* is set to be released in the fall of 2018.

KIANDRA JIMENEZ is a homeschooling mother, avid organic vegetable gardener, and artist from California. An MFA graduate (poetry and fiction) of Antioch University, Jimenez teaches poetry and fiction writing at Yavapai College. Most days she can be found searching for yellow in nature, mourning her Granma, or forcing poetry down her teenagers' and husband's throats. Kiandra recently finished *Sleep, Little Father*, her first poetry collection, and is working on her second full poetry collection.

Kz is a writer and a teaching artist and a person person from the West Side of Chicago.

E'MON LAUREN is from the South Side of Chicago. She is a Scorpio enthusiast and a firm believer in Dorothy Dandridge reincarnation. E'mon uses poetry and playwriting to explore a philosophy of hood womanism. She was named Chicago's first Youth Poet Laureate. A former Kuumba Lynx Performance Ensemble slam team member and Louder Than A Bomb champion, E'mon has performed in many venues, including the Brave New Voices International Youth Poetry Festival and the Chicago Hip Hop Theatre Fest. She was a 2016 finalist for the Gwendolyn Brooks Open Mic Award. E'mon has been published in *The BreakBeat Poets: New American Poetry in the Age of Hip-Hop*, *The Down Dirty Word*, and elsewhere. She has been featured in *Chicago Magazine*, the *Chicago Tribune*, and on WGN Radio. She is a member of Young Chicago Authors Teaching Artist Corps. Her first chapbook, *COMMANDO*, was published by Haymarket Books in the fall of 2017.

Bryan Allen Lamb

LIN-Z is a poet ternt rapper from the West Side of Chicago.

NABILA LOVELACE is a first-generation Queens native; her people hail from Trinidad and Nigeria. *Sons of Achilles*, her debut book of poems, is forthcoming from YesYes Books.

VENESSA MARCO is a 2013 third-place National Slam Champion and a finalist in the 2014 Women of the World Poetry Championship. She is an Afro-Caribbean writer pursuing her education, focusing on anthropology and creative writing, in New York City. She is a lover of Jazz and love.

ROYA MARSH, New York native, is a nationally ranked poet/educator/activist. She is the Poet in Residence with Urban Word NYC and has the dopest sneaker collection to date. Roya was 2014 Nuyorican Grand Slam Champion. She has been a finalist at the Woman of the World Poetry Slam in 2015 & 2017, in both the individual and team slam at Rustbelt 2016 and the 2017 National Poetry Slam. She has been featured in the *Village Voice, Huffington Post*, Blavity, *The Root, Button Poetry*, Def Jam's All Def Digital, Lexus Verses and Flow, and BET.

SYREETA MCFADDEN is a writer and professor of English at the Borough of Manhattan Community College, City University of New York. Her work has been featured in *New York Times Magazine, BuzzFeed, Brooklyn Magazine*, the *Guardian, Rolling Stone*, and *Storyscape Journal*. She is currently working on a collection of essays about Black Wisconsin.

Erskine Isaac

NINA ANGELA MERCER's plays include *GUTTA BEAUTIFUL; RACING MY GIRL, SALLY; ITAGUA MEJI: A ROAD & A PRAYER*; and *GYPSY & THE BULLY DOOR*. She is developing *MOTHER WIT & WATER-BORN*, a trilogy. Nina's writing is published in *Black Renaissance Noire, The Killens Review of Arts & Letters, Voices Magazine #SayHerName Edition*, and *Continuum: The Journal of African Diaspora Drama, Theatre, and Performance*. Nina is also a mother, educator, and interdisciplinary performance artist.

CIARA DARNISE MILLER, a native of Chicago, holds both an MFA and an MA in poetry and African American/African diaspora studies from Indiana University. She has published poems and academic essays in such collections and periodicals as *The Whiskey of Our Discontent, The BreakBeat Poets, Mosaic, Fjords Review, African American Review, Callaloo, Muzzle, Alice Walker: Critical Insights, Chorus*, and many more. She currently teaches Afro-American Studies at Kennedy King College, and she is the founder of Miller's Learning Center (MLC), a test-prep and career-support company with an international reach.

AJA MONET is an Afro-Cuban-Jamaican poet from East New York, Brooklyn. A graduate of Sarah Lawrence College, she was awarded the Andrea Klein Willison Prize for Poetry, established to recognize work in poetry that "effectively examines relationships among women, especially in the context of justice for everyone." She received an MFA in creative writing from the School of the Art Institute of Chicago.

YESENIA MONTILLA is an Afro-Latina poet & translator. Her poetry has appeared in *The Wide Shore*, *Prairie Schooner*, and others. She received her MFA from Drew University in poetry & poetry in translation and is a CantoMundo Fellow. *The Pink Box* is published by Willow Books and was long-listed for the Pen Open Book Award 2016.

DEBORAH D.E.E.P MOUTON, is a mother, wife, educator, and the current Poet Laureate of Houston, Texas. This seven-time National Poetry Slam Competitor and head coach of the Houston VIP Poetry Slam Team has been ranked the #2 Best Female Poet in the World. Her work has appeared in *Houston Noir*, the *Houston Chronicle*, and on such platforms as BBC, ABC, Blavity, and Upworthy.

Rachel Eliza Griffiths

ANGEL NAFIS is the author of *BlackGirl Mansion* (Red Beard Press/New School Poetics, 2012). She earned her BA at Hunter College and is an MFA candidate in poetry at Warren Wilson College. Her work has appeared in *The BreakBeat Poets*, *Buzzfeed Reader*, *Poetry*, and elsewhere. Nafis is the recipient of fellowships from Cave Canem, the Millay Colony, the Poetry Foundation, and the

National Endowment for the Arts. Founder and curator of the Greenlight
Bookstore Poetry Salon, she is also half of the ODES FOR YOU TOUR
with poet, musician, and visual artist Shira Erlichman, and with poet
Morgan Parker, she runs The Other Black Girl Collective.

NONAE of the house Pink Door, the storyteller,
the black girl sickness, the tender and blushing dyke,
first of her name, is a novice necromancer and sad girl
from the sticks. Shey is a performance poet, a 2016
Pink Door Fellow, a 2017 Watering Hole resident,
and two-time national poetry slam semi-finalist with
Beltway (DC) and Pure Ink (Buffalo) poetry slams.

NONAME (born Fatimah Warner) is an American
artist from Chicago, Illinois, who blurs the lines of
poetry and rap through the music she creates. When
she was just a senior in high school, she placed
third in Louder Than A Bomb, a poetry competi-
tion with 120 Chicago high schools in participa-
tion. She remained connected with the artists she
met at YouMedia and in 2013, her verse on Chance
the Rapper's "Lost" attracted the beginning of her large fan base, most
of whom have been following her every move since. On July 31st, 2016
Noname released her debut project entitled *Telefone* which was three years
in the making and highly anticipated by fans and media alike. Instantly the
project gained critical acclaim with a rave review by Pitchfork and landing
her praise from major outlets like *Rolling Stone, Complex,* and *Dazed &
Confused.* Noname has been hailed by *The FADER, Complex,* and *Rolling
Stone* as one of the most exciting and important new artists of 2016.

THIAHERA NURSE is from Queens, New York,
by way of Trinidad and Tobago. Her work can be
found in *The Rumpus, Callaloo, The Offing, The
Winter Tangerine,* and elsewhere. She loves her
godson, honey buns, and water. She can be found
writing quietly in her mother's house and talking to
the flowers on her block.

PORSHA O. is the 2014 Individual World Poetry Slam Champion, the 2015 National Poetry Slam Champion, and the cofounder of House Slam. She identifies as a Black, poet, dyke-god, hip-hop feminist, educator, and organizer.

TOLUWANIMI OLUWAFUNMILAYO OBI-WOLE is a Nigerian-born, Colorado-raised poet, educator, and organizer. She was Denver's first Youth Poet Laureate in 2015–2016. In 2017 she was announced as one of *The Root*'s 25 Young Futurists. She was a member of SLAM NUBA from 2015–2017, and is codirector of the Slam Nuba organization. She was a TEDx Mile High speaker and is the author of two chapbooks: *OMI EBI MI* and *How to Become a Lightning Storm*.

Rachel Eliza Griffiths

MORGAN PARKER is the author of *There Are More Beautiful Things Than Beyoncé* and *Other People's Comfort Keeps Me Up At Night*. Her work has been featured in the *New Yorker*, *Paris Review*, *New York Times*, the *Nation*, *Buzzfeed*, and elsewhere. Parker is the recipient of a 2017 NEA Literature Fellowship, winner of a Pushcart Prize, and a Cave Canem graduate fellow. She is the creator and host of *Reparations, Live!* at the Ace Hotel. With Tommy Pico, she cocurates the Poets With Attitude (PWA) reading series, and with Angel Nafis, she is The Other Black Girl Collective. She lives in Los Angeles.

RACHELLE M. PARKER has work that appears in *Tupelo Quarterly*, *Lips*, *Creations Magazine*, *New Jersey English Journal*, and the anthology *Poeming Pigeons: Poems About Food*. She is a Patricia Dobler Poetry Award 2017 Honorable Mention and the winner of the Pat Schneider Poetry Contest 2014. She was awarded fellowships from Tin House Summer Workshop Poetry, Willow Arts Alliance, and Callaloo Creative Writing at Brown University and is the poetry editor for *Peregrine*, the journal for Amherst Writers and Artists.

ALEXA PATRICK is a poet and singer from
Connecticut. She is a graduate of American
University, where she was a two-time member
and coach of their College Unions Poetry Slam
Invitational slam team. She is also a teaching artist for
Split This Rock in Washington, DC, and the Center
for Creative Youth at Wesleyan University.

Nicholas Nichols

XANDRIA PHILLIPS is a poet and Cave Canem
fellow based in Chicago. Her chapbook *Reasons For
Smoking* won the 2016 *Seattle Review* chapbook
contest judged by Claudia Rankine. Find her work
at *The Offing, The Journal, Nashville Review, Ninth
Letter Online, Scalawag*, and elsewhere. For more,
visit xandriaphillips.com.

NATALIE ROSE RICHARDSON is a gradu-
ate of the University of Chicago and a fellow at the
Rebuild Foundation on Chicago's South Side. Her
work has appeared or is forthcoming in *Poetry, Arts
& Letters*, and *The Adroit Journal*, among others.
She has received awards from the Poetry Society of
America and the Davis Projects for Peace. She lives
on Chicago's South Side.

BRITTANY ROGERS is a poet, mother, educa-
tor, and proud Hufflepuff. Brittany is an editor for
wusgood.black, a literary magazine that highlights
urban writers. She has work published in *Vinyl
Poetry and Prose*, Gramma Press, *Tinderbox Poetry*,
and *FreezeRay Poetry*. She is a fellow of VONA/
Voices and Pink Door Writing Retreat.

SIMONE SAVANNAH is a poet from Columbus,
Ohio. She earned a PhD in creative writing from
the University of Kansas. Her work is forthcoming
or has appeared in *Blackberry, Big Lucks, Powder
Keg, Apogee, GlitterMOB, The Fem*, and *The Pierian*.
Her chapbook *Like Kansas* is forthcoming from Big
Lucks in 2018.

RJ Eldridge

DIAMOND JANESE SHARP is a poet and writer from Chicago. Her work has been featured on Chicago Public Radio and published in *Lenny*, *Pitchfork*, and *PANK*, among others. Diamond is the features editor at *Rookie*. She is an alumna of Wellesley College.

ALEXIS SMITHERS is a queer, Black creator on the East Coast. They currently work for Autostraddle. They are a 2015 Pink Door Fellow, 2016 Lambda Literary Young Adult Fiction Emerging Writer, and 2018 Udacity Grow With Google Scholarship Recipient. You can find them on Twitter at @ DangerLove12.

BIANCA LYNNE SPRIGGS is an award-winning poet and multidisciplinary artist currently based in Athens, Ohio, where she is an assistant professor of English at Ohio University. She is the author of four collections of poetry, most recently *Call Her by Her Name* (Northwestern University Press, 2016) and *The Galaxy is a Dance Floor* (Argos Books, 2016). You can learn more about her work at biancaspriggs.com.

EBONY STEWART is an international touring performance artist, writer, and playwright. The 2017 Women of the World Poetry Slam Co-Champion. Featured in the *Texas Observer*, *For Harriet*, *Teen Vogue*, *EASTside Magazine*, and *The Agenda: working for LGBT economic equality*. Author of *The Queen's Glory & the Pussy's Box* and *Love Letters to Balled Fists*. Winning playwright of three B. Iden Payne Awards for Outstanding Lead Actress in a Drama (2015, 2017), Best Original Script, and winner of the Austin Critics' Table David Mark Cohen New Play Award. Ebony Stewart is #storyoftheblackgirlwinning.

MARIAHADESSA EKERE TALLIE is the author of *Karma's Footsteps* (Flipped Eye), *Dear Continuum: Letters to a Poet Crafting Liberation* (Grand Concourse Press), and *Strut* (Agape Editions). Her work has been widely published, and she has traveled three continents reading it and teaching writing. Her work is the subject of the film *I Leave My Colors Everywhere*. Mariahadessa is the mother of three galaxies who look like daughters. www.ekeretallie.com.

Hailing from the Bronx, **CRYSTAL VALENTINE** is a nationally and internationally acclaimed spoken word artist, activist, and educator. She is the winner of the 2015 and 2013 College Unions Poetry Slam Invitational, the second place winner of the National Poetry Slam and the ninth ranked poet by way of the Woman of the World Poetry Slam and the Individual World Poetry Slam. Crystal has traveled across seas performing on platforms in Paris, Mexico, Brazil, South Africa, and elsewhere. She was named *Glamour Magazine*'s 2016 College Woman of the Year, *Teen Vogue*'s Rising Young Black Thought Leader, and was the recipient of the National Conference of College Women Student Leaders Woman's Distinction Award. A Callaloo Fellow, 2015 New York City Youth Poet Laureate, and author of her first book, *Not Everything Is a Eulogy* (Penmanship Books), Crystal's work has been featured on programming for MSNBC, Blavity, Button Poetry, *Huffington Post*, BET, CNN, the *New York Daily News,* and more. She earned her BA in psychology at New York University, where she is returning as a Goldwater Fellow and MFA candidate in poetry.

NIKKI WALLSCHLAEGER's work has been featured in the *Nation, Georgia Review, Boston Review, Denver Quarterly, Witness*, the PoetryNow podcast through the Poetry Foundation, and elsewhere. She is the author of the full-length collections *Houses* (Horseless Press, 2015) and *Crawlspace* (Bloof, 2017) as well as the graphic chapbook *I*

Hate Telling You How I Really Feel from Bloof Books (2016). She lives in Wisconsin.

MAYA WASHINGTON is a poet, actor, filmmaker, and arts educator. She holds a BA from the University of Southern California and an MFA from Hamline University; her writing has appeared in literary journals and anthologies and has garnered fellowships or awards from the Minnesota State Arts Board, Jerome Foundation, and others. Her award-winning narrative and documentary films have a global reach, most recently in Hong Kong, Rome, and Budapest. themayawashington.com.

LAUREN WHITEHEAD is a writer, performer, and MFA recipient in dramaturgy (Columbia University). She writes in several forms including poetry, nonfiction, and drama. Her work has been published in *Apogee, Winter Tangerine, HEArt Online*, and selected anthologies. Lauren has performed in venues around the country, notably the Apollo Theater and the Kennedy Center. She is a Sundance Theater Lab Fellow and she teaches advanced playwriting and dramaturgy at the New School. More info: laurenawhitehead.com.

CANDACE G. WILEY was born in South Carolina; graduated from Bowie State University, an HBCU in Maryland; from Clemson University; from the University of South Carolina; and is a Fulbright Fellow. She is a founding director of The Watering Hole, which builds Harlem Renaissance spaces in the New Contemporary South. Wiley is now at the Fine Arts Work Center in Provincetown, Massachusetts. Her work has appeared in *Best American Poetry 2015, Prairie Schooner, pluck!*, and *Jasper*, among others.

About Haymarket Books

Haymarket Books is a radical, independent, nonprofit book publisher based in Chicago.

Our mission is to publish books that contribute to struggles for social and economic justice. We strive to make our books a vibrant and organic part of social movements and the education and development of a critical, engaged, international left.

We take inspiration and courage from our namesakes, the Haymarket martyrs, who gave their lives fighting for a better world. Their 1886 struggle for the eight-hour day—which gave us May Day, the international workers' holiday—reminds workers around the world that ordinary people can organize and struggle for their own liberation. These struggles continue today across the globe—struggles against oppression, exploitation, poverty, and war.

Since our founding in 2001, Haymarket Books has published more than five hundred titles. Radically independent, we seek to drive a wedge into the risk-averse world of corporate book publishing. Our authors include Noam Chomsky, Arundhati Roy, Rebecca Solnit, Angela Y. Davis, Howard Zinn, Amy Goodman, Wallace Shawn, Mike Davis, Winona LaDuke, Ilan Pappé, Richard Wolff, Dave Zirin, Keeanga-Yamahtta Taylor, Nick Turse, Dahr Jamail, David Barsamian, Elizabeth Laird, Amira Hass, Mark Steel, Avi Lewis, Naomi Klein, and Neil Davidson. We are also the trade publishers of the acclaimed Historical Materialism Book Series and of Dispatch Books.

Also Available
from Haymarket Books

1989, The Number
Kevin Coval and Nate Marshall

Before the Next Bomb Drops: Rising Up from Brooklyn to Palestine
Remi Kanazi

The BreakBeat Poets: New American Poetry in the Age of Hip-Hop
Edited by Kevin Coval, Quraysh Ali Lansana, and Nate Marshall

Electric Arches
Eve L. Ewing

From #BlackLivesMatter to Black Liberation
Keeanga-Yamahtta Taylor

My Mother Was a Freedom Fighter
Aja Monet

A People's History of Chicago
Kevin Coval, Foreword by Chance the Rapper

Inauguration
Idris Goodwin and Nico Wilkinson

How We Get Free: Black Feminism and the Combahee River Collective
Edited by Keeanga-Yamahtta Taylor

A Beautiful Ghetto
by Devin Allen, Introduction by Keeanga-Yamahtta Taylor and D. Watkins

Undivided Rights: Women of Color Organizing for Reproductive Justice
Marlene Gerber Fried, Elena Gutiérrez, Loretta Ross, and Jael Silliman

The Whiskey of our Discontent: Gwendolyn Brooks as Conscience and Change Agent
Edited by Quraysh Ali Lansana and Georgia A. Popoff, Introduction by Sonia Sanchez